HUMILITAS

HUMILITAS

A LOST KEY TO **LIFE, LOVE,** AND **LEADERSHIP**

JOHN DICKSON

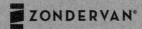

ZONDERVAN.com/
AUTHORTRACKER
follow your favorite authors

ZONDERVAN

Humilitas
Copyright © 2011 by John Dickson

This title is also available as a Zondervan ebook.
Visit www.zondervan.com/ebooks.

This title is also available in a Zondervan audio edition.
Visit www.zondervan.fm.

Requests for information should be addressed to:

Zondervan, *Grand Rapids, Michigan* 49530

Library of Congress Cataloging-in-Publication Data

Dickson, John, 1967 – .
    Humilitas : a lost key to life, love, and leadership/ John Dickson.
      p. cm.
    ISBN 978-0-310-32862-9 (hardcover)
    1. Humility – Religious aspects – Christianity. I. Title.
    BV4647.H8D53 2010
    241'.4 – dc22   2010039774

All Scripture quotations, unless otherwise indicated, are taken from the Holy
Bible, *New International Version®, NIV®*. Copyright © 1973, 1978, 1984 by
Biblica, Inc.™ Used by permission of Zondervan. All rights reserved worldwide.

Any Internet addresses (websites, blogs, etc.) and telephone numbers printed
in this book are offered as a resource. They are not intended in any way to be
or imply an endorsement by Zondervan, nor does Zondervan vouch for the
content of these sites and numbers for the life of this book.

Cover design: Rob Monacelli
Interior design: Matthew VanZomeren and Ben Fetterley

Printed in the United States of America

---

11 12 13 14 15 16 /DCI/ 19 18 17 16 15 14 13 12 11 10 9 8 7 6 5 4 3 2

For
Paul Barnett,
Bruce Robinson,
and Richard Grellman,
mentors,
who know more about this subject than I do
but would never presume to write a book about it

Contents

Acknowledgments

Many thanks:

to Nigel and Lisa Champion for giving this material its first audience at Filex 2008

to Kate Wilcox, Jenny Glen, Scott Walters, Richard Shumack, and my wife, Buff, for valuable research assistance

and to my St Andrew's family for patiently allowing me to neglect them

while I wrote a book on humility

Introduction

Humility and How I Achieved It

THERE IS AN OBVIOUS CONUNDRUM FACING THE writer and readers of a book on humility. Does the author think he has attained this difficult virtue? If so, he almost certainly hasn't. If not, why is he writing a book on the topic?

Strangely, the dilemma doesn't seem to apply to other virtues. I could probably get away with writing a book on compassion in organizations or discipline in relationships or generosity in public life without raising eyebrows. But there is something about advocating humility that makes people, especially the author, feel a little uncomfortable (obviously, not uncomfortable enough for me not to write the book and for you not to pick it up, but you know what I mean). Humility stands alone among the virtues in that as soon as you think you have it, you probably don't. And, yet, the reverse does not follow. *Not* thinking yourself humble is no indication that you are. You might be right! Both the arrogant and the humble are unlikely to think of themselves as humble. So, how could you ever know if you have attained the virtue? This is not the only paradox we will meet in our discussion.

Let me tell you how I see myself as the author of a book on humility. I am a dominance-leaning, achievement-focused, driven personality who has accidentally fallen in love with an intriguing ancient virtue. I say this not as a cute way to introduce a book on the topic. It is the reality. From the start of my love-hate relationship with humility, friends and close colleagues frequently noted a certain irony that *Dickson* had become interested in the theme. I will never forget the comment of my best friend of thirty-five years when I told him I was involved in a research project at Macquarie University's ancient history department on *the origins of humility in Western ethical thought.* He quipped, "Well, John, at least you have the objective distance from the subject!" (One of the keys to developing humility is spending more time with friends who speak plainly.)

I was recently confronted with proof of this "objective distance". I work with a not-for-profit think tank and media company. As part of my professional development last year I submitted to the well-known DISC analysis of behavioural patterns. Developed fifty years ago by psychologists from Harvard University and refined constantly since then, DISC assesses people along four quadrants: dominance, influence, steadiness and conscientiousness. We all display features of these four descriptors, but each of us *tends* toward one more than the others.

I won't keep you guessing my own tendency: "high dominance with an intensity score of 26.5 out of 28". Many leaders probably fall into this category. They might also think of it as a badge of honour. I did too for a few minutes, until I read the detailed report. Unfortunately, dominance does not mean high-achieving, competent or fit to lead. There is no formal connection between this quadrant and effectiveness. It just means that, whatever their capabilities and principles, dominance individuals like to assert viewpoints and control situations. (I suspect many serial killers would score high in Dominance.) To quote the report—as much of it as my wife will allow me to publish:

> John, you are high in the Dominance (D) dimension. As a result, you are likely to be focused on shaping your environment by overcoming opposition to achieve results ... As someone with a Result-Oriented Pattern, you tend to be a quick thinker who displays self-confidence. [*No problem so far, right?*] You are usually determined and persistent. You may frequently display a dominant personality that increases the odds you will be viewed as forceful and direct. [*Then comes the slug.*] Your tendency to be fiercely independent may frequently give you an air of self-importance. Adding to this perception is that you may often become impatient or haughty ... Rather than overstep your boundaries or exceed your authority, it might be beneficial for you to verbalise your reasoning. Explaining your rationale may frequently prevent conflicts from arising. An additional way to boost your efficiency would be to increase your patience and improve your sense of humility.[1]

For several years now I have been trying to improve my "sense of humility". In fact, for the last three years it has been #3 of my eleven yearly goals. I've seen about as much progress here as I have with goal #11: "learn to cook three nice meals." I've nearly perfected the traditional Indonesian dish Gado-gado, but that's about it. It was following my DISC assessment that I emailed my publisher with what I hoped they would recognize as a joke. "Stop press," I wrote, "I've come up with the perfect title for the new book: *Humility and How I Achieved It.*" Within hours I got a reply in the form of a brilliant book-cover design based on the idea. It featured a huge smiling image of me and multiple endorsements—from me—and was accompanied by a "marketing rationale": "We feel strongly that it represents your brand and meets our marketing and consumer objectives ... Overall, the cover, title, and photo really capture the essence of your message. It will, no doubt, stop people in their tracks." It was a humorous, if slightly disturbing, reminder of my objective distance from this subject.

I do not claim to have attained humility, but I can say I have thought long and hard about it and have grown to love the virtue for its aesthetic qualities and its practical benefits. This book unpacks both.

CHAPTER 1

Thesis

What Is Humility and Why Does It Matter?

I SPEAK AS AN OUTSIDER ON THE SUBJECT OF
leadership. I have become aware in writing this book just
how large an industry the leadership track is. The books
and journals on the theme would take a lifetime to review.
I have done what I can to learn from leadership academics
like Jim Collins at Stanford, John P. Kotter and Joseph L.
Badaracco at Harvard and Simon Walker at Oxford. I've
read some of the practical reflections of leaders like Charles
Farkas of Bain & Company, Thomas Teal of the Boston
Consulting Group and the forever-famous guru of leadership, Stephen R. Covey. But I remain a leadership hack with
no claim to understand the intricacies of corporate management, let alone contribute to the sophisticated conversation
going on in the field.

What I hope to bring to this discussion is *historical perspective*. That's my training: history — in particular, ancient
history. I realize that might not sound particularly relevant

to the executive who wants up-to-date, ahead-of-the-pack information on creating organizational momentum, managing relationships, setting goals, communicating change and so on, but my defense in this case is the one I offer whenever someone asks me the point of studying history. Learning history (and especially learning *from* it) is the ultimate exercise in democracy. By it you give a voice not just to the "blip" we call the twenty-first-century West but to the whole human family, ancient and modern. You allow the dead to cast a vote in the discussions and decisions of the present.

The value of such learning from history is hard to overstate. Our contemporary society may have eclipsed the past in terms of science, medicine and technology but in other areas I reckon we are only "about average" compared to the ancients. In some things we are "well below par". You only have to read Siddhartha Gautama, the Buddha, on the art of concentration (fifth century BC),[1] or Aristotle on communication theory (fourth century),[2] or Seneca on ethics (first century AD),[3] or Plutarch on the complexities of friendship (second century),[4] or St Augustine on human nature (fifth century),[5] or Heloise on romantic love (twelfth century)[6] or William of Ockham on natural human rights (fourteenth century)[7] to discover two things: first, there are few truly new ideas in the world; second, real wisdom for life and leadership is found not just in the latest issue of the *Harvard Business Review* (as helpful as it is) but in opening yourself up to centuries of human thinking on these and other topics. The reader of history is the ultimate pollster, canvassing the opinion of the entire human family.

With all of that said, please don't imagine that *Humili-tas* is some ethereal call to plumb the depths of history and philosophy. Despite the pretentious Latin-root title, this is an essentially practical book. I will be drawing on ideas and authors long gone, but only in passing and mainly to flag that my best thoughts are secondhand. Apart from a section on the *origins* of the virtue of humility in the Western ethical tradition, which readers should feel free to skip over, most of what follows is a straightforward attempt to describe the importance of humility for contemporary life, love and leadership and to outline its very real benefits.

The Thesis

My thesis is simple: *The most influential and inspiring people are often marked by humility.* True greatness, in other words, frequently goes hand in hand with a virtue that, on the face of it, might be thought to curb achievement and mute influence. In fact, I believe it does the opposite.

I will define humility in a moment, but it's worth noting the way it pops up in some unexpected places. Many readers will know the work of Jim Collins, the Stanford University business analyst and author of the best-selling *Good to Great.* He conducted a five-year study exploring what turns good companies into great ones. He defined a "great" company as one that experienced a turn-around in which it financially outperformed the market trend by at least three times for a fifteen-year period. One classic example is

Jim Collins, 2005

Gillette, best known for shaving products. Between 1980 and 1995 the company enjoyed cumulative stock returns 7.39 times greater than the general stock market. Only eleven companies in the US made Collins's "great" category. Most notable were those that didn't make the cut, including Coca-Cola, Johnson & Johnson, Wal-Mart and General Electric, companies that only outperformed the market by 2.5 times.

Many observers were surprised to learn that one of the key factors in all eleven good-to-great companies during the growth phase was what Collins described as Level 5 Leadership — that is, leadership marked by two characteristics: steely determination and an attitude of humility. Collins records the puzzlement of his research team at the consistency of this finding:

> We were surprised, shocked really, to discover the type of leadership required for turning a good company into a great one. Compared to high-profile leaders with big personalities who make headlines and become celebrities, the good-to-great leaders seem to have come from Mars. Self-effacing, quiet, reserved even shy — these leaders are a paradoxical blend of personal humility and professional

will. They are more like Lincoln and Socrates than Patton or Caesar.[8]

Collins's 2009 book *How the Mighty Fall* bears out the flipside—when successful companies become arrogant, it often spells their downfall.[9]

Then there is General Stanley McChrystal, number two in *Time* magazine's "Person of the Year" for 2009. Before his removal for unfavourable remarks about the Obama administration, he was commander of all forces in Afghanistan and one of the most celebrated leaders in US military history. A Harvard graduate, he runs over ten kilometers daily, eats one meal a day and sleeps four hours a night. We might say he is a high achiever. During a surprisingly frank press conference held in London shortly after his appointment as commander, McChrystal offered an intriguing, one-word summary of his approach to the insurgency in Afghanistan:

> I have found in my experience that the best answers and approaches may be counter-intuitive. The opposite of what it seems you ought to do is what ought to be done. So, when I'm asked the question, What approach should we take in Afghanistan? I say, humility.

We are left wondering exactly what humble counter-insurgency looks like—though I suppose he meant understanding and serving the Afghan people will go a long way toward undermining the influence of the Taliban. But I was truly fascinated to watch his remarks and to observe the way he paused afterward for emphasis. It was as if an oracle had been spoken. The unwinnable war can be won through humility. Humility appears in some unlikely places.

General McChrystal is right to describe this idea as "counterintuitive". Readers might already be asking, How can influence be exerted and enemies be overcome through humility? Surely, what is needed is forcefulness! It all depends how we define the word.

General Stanley McChrystal delivers a speech in London, October 1, 2009.

AP Images

What Is Humility?

Humility does not mean humiliation, even though both words are offspring of a single Latin parent (*humilitas*). Nor does it mean being a doormat for others, having low self-esteem or curbing your strengths and achievements. Collins's work reminds us it is possible to be humble, iron-willed and successful, and they frequently go together. Muhammad Ali was wrong when he once quipped, "At home I'm a nice guy: but I don't want the world to know. Humble people, I've found, don't get very far."[10]

Having strong opinions is no hindrance to humility either. One of the failings of contemporary Western culture is to confuse conviction with arrogance. I will explore this further in chapter 10, where I suggest that humility, rightly understood, is a potential antidote to the hateful political and religious rhetoric we often hear: Left versus Right, Christian versus Muslim and so on. I want to argue that the solution to ideological discord is not "tolerance" in the postmodern form we frequently find it, the bland affirmation of all viewpoints as equally true and valid but an ability to profoundly disagree with others and deeply honour them at the same time. It should be entirely possible for Christians to reject Islamic doctrine as invalid and untrue — to maintain theological conviction, in other words — without diminishing their capacity to honour Muslims as fellow members of the human family. Likewise, the political Right should be able to disagree with the Left, and vice versa, without descending into name-calling, backbiting and worse.

So what is humility if it isn't surrendering our convictions, strengths and achievements? The etymology of the word is helpful but requires some explanation to avoid misunderstanding. Several ancient cultures have contributed to Western culture generally. The influential British political philosopher John Macmurray put it like this: "Three old civilizations have been mixed together to form the culture of which we are the heirs — the Hebrew, the Greek and the Roman, a religious, an artistic and an organizing, administrative or scientific civilization. These three streams of old experience have never really fused."[11] This is no less true of the story of humility.

I will say more about this in chapters 5 and 6. For now I just want to point out that the peculiar Western meaning of "humility" derives from the usage of the Hebrew-speaking Jews, Latin-speaking Romans and the Greeks, in particular Greek-speaking Christians of the first century. In all three languages the word used to describe humility means "low", as in *low to the ground*: the Hebrew *anawa*, the Greek *tapeinos*, and the already-familiar Latin *humilitas*. Used negatively, these terms mean *to be put low*, that is, "to be humiliated". Positively, they mean *to lower yourself* or "to be humble".

The two uses are radically different. One is the awful experience of being conquered or shamed, and this was the dominant usage of the term in ancient times. The other is the noble choice to redirect your power in service of others. This became the dominant usage only late in the Roman period (second to fifth centuries AD) and for reasons I will explain in chapter 6.

We are now in a position to define the term as I will use it throughout the book. Humility is *the noble choice to forgo your status, deploy your resources or use your influence for the good of others before yourself.* More simply, you could say the humble person is marked by *a willingness to hold power in service of others.*

There are three key thoughts in this definition. First, humility presupposes your *dignity*. The one being humble acts from a height, so to speak, as the "lowering" etymology makes clear. True humility assumes the dignity or strength of the one possessing the virtue, which is why it should not be confused with having low self-esteem or being a doormat for others. In fact, I would go so far as to say that it is impossible to be humble in the real sense without a healthy sense of your own worth and abilities. Mark Strom, a fellow historian and proper leadership analyst, puts it well:

> Wise leaders hold nobility with humility. Overbearing ego and debilitating self-abasement are generally avoided in all wisdom traditions. Many traditions call for balance. I would suggest a further step, also found in the ancient wisdom writings: that you look beyond balance, that you embrace the paradox of strength in weakness to find your true weight as a leader.[12]

Second, humility is *willing*. It is a choice. Otherwise, it is humiliation.

Finally, humility is *social*. It is not a private act of self-deprecation—banishing proud thoughts, refusing to talk about your achievements and so on. I would call this simple "modesty". But humility is about redirecting of your powers, whether physical, intellectual, financial or structural, *for the sake of others*. One of the earliest Greek texts on this topic, written about AD 60 to the Roman colony of Philippi, puts it perfectly: "In a humble frame of mind regard one another as if better than yourselves—each of you taking care not only of your own needs but also of the needs of others."[13] Humility is more about how I treat others than how I think about myself.

Let me illustrate the three aspects of humility with an example of the virtue. There are so many to choose from. If this were my history of religions class, I might mention the Indian prince who, despite the comforts of his position, turned his significant intellect to the task of overcoming suffering. Or I might talk about the Galilean rabbi who influenced Western history probably more than any other individual but who epitomized humility, once even washing his students' feet like a slave as an object lesson in leadership.

My example is a sporting one. Again, the options are endless. Think of Roger Federer, at one time the world's number one tennis player, who seems incapable of winning or losing without praising his opponent; or five-times all-China martial arts champion and Hollywood Kung Fu star Jet Li, who now uses his fame and fortune to relieve Asia's poor through the ONE Foundation. My favourite illustration, however, comes from last century from the boxing industry, an industry usually associated with other-person-centredness of a very different kind. I haven't been able to verify the story but I hope I have at least the basic details correct.

Three young men hopped on a bus in Detroit in the 1930s and tried to pick a fight with a lone man sitting at the back of the vehicle. They insulted him. He didn't respond. They turned up the heat of the insults. He said nothing. Eventually, the stranger stood up. He was bigger than they had estimated from his seated position — much bigger. He reached into his pocket, handed them his business card and walked off the bus and then on his way. As the bus drove on the young men gathered around the card to read the words: *Joe Louis. Boxer.* They had just tried to pick a fight with the man who would be Heavyweight Boxing Champion of the World from 1937 to 1949, the number one boxer of all time, according to the International Boxing Research Organization (second on the list is Muhammad Ali).[14] They apparently said of Louis that he could knock out a horse with one punch. I struggle to think how he got that reputation, but the point is simple. Here is a man of immense power and skill, capable of defending his honour with a single, devastating blow. Yet, he chooses to forgo his status and hold his power for others—in this case, for some very fortunate young men.

Joe Louis posed for this photo January 23, 1945, just before giving a bag-punching exhibition for soldiers, who were eager to see the "Brown Bomber" in action.

This story is emblematic of Louis's whole life. Raised in poverty by former slave parents, Louis never forgot his lowly beginnings and saw his successes as opportunities to give back something of what he had received. According to a *PBS* special on the fighter, Louis was generous to a fault, lavishing family members with cash and homes, handing out twenty-dollar bills to anyone who asked and even paying back the city of Detroit for all the welfare monies his family had received in the early years.[15] The man was no saint and, like many in his situation, he ran into financial troubles later in life. But he is remembered not only for his unparalleled boxing achievements but also for his willingness to hold power in service of others, for his humility.

To return to my thesis: in this book I am suggesting that humility, rightly understood, has often marked the most influential and inspiring people in history, whether religious figures like Buddha and Jesus, social activists like William Wilberforce, Mahatma Gandhi and Nelson Mandela, or some of the "most remarkable CEO's of the century"[16] detailed in Jim Collins's research: Darwin E. Smith of Kimberly-Clark, Colman Mockler of Gillette and Ken Iverson of the steel giant Nucor.

Leaving aside such high achievers, I contend that some of the most influential people in our daily lives exert their influence with humility. It is certainly true in my case. I think of my inconspicuous Year 5 teacher, Mr. Bingham. He was hardly an "authority figure" in the school — plenty of teachers were louder, funnier and scarier than he was — but for some reason I still find myself thinking fondly about his gentle fatherly tone and endless patience with this disruptive eleven-year-old.

Or there's my good friend Professor Bruce Robinson, an international authority on respiratory disease from the University of Western Australia. At home and among friends, he is unassuming in the extreme. He is happier reclining on the couch in shorts with beer in hand, quizzing others about their opinions on life (especially if they come from outside his educated middle-class circle) than he is standing before the medical world informing peers of his research team's latest discoveries. As I said to some of his friends at a dinner party recently, he is one of the few people in my life whose opinions I find *almost* as compelling as my own! Influence through humility is a key theme of this book.

Let me be clear that I am not saying that humility automatically makes someone great. Plenty of humble people achieve little more than deep and enduring relationships (which, come to think of it, is probably life's truest test of success). Nor am I saying you can't ascend "the heights" without humility. We all know high achievers who seem perfectly happy maintaining their objective distance from the virtue. What I am saying is that humility enhances the ordinary and makes the great even greater. Whether you are an average Joe or Joanne trying to make a difference in your neighborhood or a corporate leader, football coach, military commander, school teacher or parent keen to enhance your impact on those in your care, my aim is to convince you of the logic, beauty and benefits of the ancient virtue of *humilitas*.

CHAPTER 2

Leadership

What It Is and How Humility Fits In

THERE ARE AS MANY DEFINITIONS OF LEADERSHIP
as there are books on the topic. As I said earlier, I am a leadership hack with no illusions about contributing to the vast
and thoughtful literature on the subject. But it is probably
important to explain to readers how I think about leadership, if for no other reason than to *locate* my discussion of
humility within it. Nothing I say below will be new, but
hopefully, the framework I describe will clarify for readers
why I place such a premium on the virtue.

What Is Leadership?

I doubt it is controversial to describe leadership as *the art
of inspiring others in a team to contribute their best toward a
goal*. We might quibble over the wording — and I am calling
this a description rather than a definition — but I suspect

most would agree with the three main aspects of leadership identified here.

Art. Leadership is more an art than a science. This is why there are as many leadership styles, books and courses as there are forms of art. What worked for Emperor Augustus as he unified the Roman world to become its "first man" or *princeps* (in 27 BC) does not necessarily work for Rick Warren as he pastors one of America's largest churches. There will be some overlap of function even in such different roles, but overall, leadership tends to be *flexible*, depending on the goals of the organization, and *intuitive,* depending on the personalities involved. That is to say, it is an art form.

Others. The second part of the description is equally straightforward. Leadership is fundamentally about others. It hardly needs to be said that a leader is not just a high-achieving performer with a high-D personality. More than a star, a leader is able to move members of a team toward the goals of the organization. Great footballers—I mean the game that actually uses the "foot" most of the time—do not always make great coaches.

Perhaps the most striking example in recent times is Diego Maradona, one of the most amazing players of all time. I remember first watching him when he helped Argentina's junior squad win the Youth World Cup of 1979. In 1986 he repeated the achievement with the adult national team. In the quarter-final of that tournament he scored what is often called "the goal of the century" (worth You-Tubing). Football fans were mesmerized by the way the ball seemed magnetically attracted to his feet as he weaved his way around the opposition before finding the back of the net over thirty-four times in his international career.

Despite his brilliance on the field, Maradona's elevation to become the head coach and manager of the national team of Argentina from 2008 has not been glorious. Team performances have been erratic, including a 6 – 1 defeat to Bolivia, equaling Argentina's worst ever performance, and climaxing most recently in a 4 – 0 routing by Germany in the 2010 World Cup quarter finals. The world governing body for football, FIFA, also suspended him for two months

AP Images

Argentine soccer player Diego Maradona, left, tries to go past England's Trevor Steven, during the World Cup quarter final match, in Mexico City, on June 22, 1986.

following "abusive language" at a press conference. Nothing will take away from Maradona my playing hero; but the jury was divided on Maradona the manager-coach. Just before I finished this book, the Argentina Football Association announced it would not be renewing Maradona's contract.

What is true in sport is equally true in academia and business. There is no guarantee that the most talented individual will be an inspiring leader, for leadership is about "aligning people"—to use Professor J. P. Kotter's language, "motivating and inspiring" them.[1] "The real power of effective leadership," writes Brigadier Jim Wallace, former head of Australian special forces, "is maximising other people's potential."[2]

Goal. The third obvious aspect of leadership is that it is oriented toward a clear goal. There is something fundamentally aspirational and idealistic about leadership. Those who lead organizations are constantly straining toward the greater realization of an agreed outcome, whether a financial bottom line, a military victory, social reform or academic excellence. This is why Kotter repeatedly emphasizes that leadership at its core "is about coping with change".[3] Not change for change's sake, but movement toward a goal necessarily involves change. Whereas managers "cope with complexity", he says, responding to the week-by-week operational details of the organization, leaders look to the months and years ahead and imagine, communicate and strategize the organization's transformation. This idealistic dimension of the leader is well described by Simon Walker, who teaches leadership at Oxford University:

Most leaders are to some extent idealists. They have a desire for things to be different, to be better. Thus, the leader lives all the time with a discrepancy between the world that she wants (and wants others) to inhabit and the world she (and others) actually do inhabit. Psychologists call this condition "cognitive dissonance"—there is a discord between the reality and the ideal … Most people deal with the cognitive dissonance fairly effectively simply by choosing to look away from the ideal. They come to tolerate the reality by avoiding the evidence, by filtering the data they receive. They fabricate a world in which the discrepancy is less. The leader, however, is motivated by a desire to hold on to the ideal—indeed, it is the ideal that drives her. Accordingly, she commits herself to a journey that will inevitably lead her into a dissonance between the reality and the ideal, a tension that she refuses, until she gives up leading, to deny or suppress.[4]

Tools of leadership

If leadership can be described as the art of inspiring others in a team to contribute their best to a goal, what are the "tools" at the leader's disposal? Again, I doubt there will be much disagreement when I say that there are basically four.

Ability. Leaders tend to be people who have excelled in some important part of the organization's business. While it is true that a "star performer" does not necessarily make a good leader, it is equally true that good leaders nearly always have a decent track record in some area relevant to the company. Sir Alex Ferguson was no Maradona when he played for Scottish clubs Dunfermline and Rangers, but he could not have become one of the most successful manager-coaches in British football history, leading Manchester United to unparalleled victories over the last twenty-five years, without some significant earlier achievements as a player.

The same point can be made about a military and political leader like Dwight D. Eisenhower, a business executive like Coca-Cola's Muhtar Kent or a university president like Princeton's Shirley Tilghman. These people had excellent track records in their specific fields (without necessarily being technical stars) before rising to the most important positions of leadership in their respective industries. Good leaders will always have some observable ability that commands respect from the team.

Authority. What I mean by authority is the structural powers handed to leaders by an organization — the power to hire and fire, set directions, approve budgets and overrule colleagues where there is disagreement. In some ways, this is the least useful tool for effective, long-term leadership (unless you are Kim Jong-Il or the emperor of Rome). Heavy reliance on authority is often the result of laziness, since enforcing is much easier than energizing and creating momentum. It also quickly transforms *leadership* into *rule* — which is not the same thing.

Nevertheless, authority remains part of the reality of leadership and should not be overlooked. It is a bit like parental authority. Every mum and dad hope to direct their kids without imposing excessive rules and threats, but they also know that sometimes taking charge of a situation is an act of kindness and in the best interests of the family. Leaders sometimes need to do the same. Where the analogy breaks down, however, is that whereas the authority of mums and dads is *inherent*—an intrinsic and automatic reality of the parent-child relationship—the powers of a military commander, CEO or university president are all *conferred*. They are granted to the leader by the organization. They are therefore extrinsic privileges and should be viewed as such. In other words, unlike "ability" (discussed above) and "persuasion" and "example" (discussed below), authority does not belong to the leader. This alone makes it a secondary tool of leadership.

Persuasion. Good leaders tend not to rely on structural authority but instead have a knack of winning people over to their vision of things. I have been surprised and delighted to see how much of the leadership literature emphasizes this point. In the *Harvard Business Review on Leadership*, a compendium of scholarly reflections on the topic, virtually every chapter stresses the role of communication. Unless a leader can convey a vision and convince team members of its worth, leadership is just hard work.

Al Zeinen led shaving giant Gillette through its most successful years following the death of Colman Mockler in 1991. He was renowned for constant travel. Why? Certainly not because he enjoyed the jet-setting lifestyle, but because he wanted to make sure that his vision was being communicated across the 34,000 employees worldwide. "I travel because that's where the people are," he says. "I travel because I want to be sure that people who are making the decisions in, say, Argentina have the same reference base as

I do for the company. I want to make sure they are all using the same ground rules I would use. I want to see if they have the same objectives."[5]

Persuading people about the "reference base", "ground rules" and "objectives" of a company's vision is central to leadership. Few would doubt that persuasion was an important part of Barack Obama's rise to power. I know that some now suggest he was "all talk and no action", but only the most one-eyed commentator could deny the man's extraordinary ability to make people believe in his vision. After watching some Obama speeches during the 2008 election campaign, my fourteen-year-old boy was about ready to move to the US.

Example. This is a deliberately broad category that includes everything from the leader's listening ear to his work ethic to a courteous tone toward subordinates. Leaders underestimate the power of example at their peril. I suspect things have improved since Stephen R. Covey's 1989 classic *The Seven Habits of Highly Effective People*, but it is worth recalling his account of two hundred years of American writing on leadership and achievement: "I began to feel more and more that much of the success literature of the past 50 years was superficial. It was filled with social image consciousness, techniques and quick fixes," he laments.[6]

By contrast, almost all of the relevant literature of the first 150 years (from 1776) emphasized the importance of example or character. It "focused on what could be called the *Character Ethic* as the foundation of success — things like integrity, humility, fidelity, temperance, courage, justice, patience, industry, simplicity, modesty, and the Golden Rule." This Character Ethic, Covey says, "taught that there are basic principles of effective living, and that people can only experience true success and enduring happiness as they learn and integrate these principles into their basic character."[7]

Character or example is central to leadership. Unless a leader is trusted by the team, she will not get the best out of them. This is because all organizations, even hugely hierarchical ones like the military, are still *communities of people in relationship.* There is no avoiding the "human" in leadership. In fact, this is the basic premise of my book. Since life is fundamentally about relationships, the relational virtues such as humility, compassion, trustworthiness and so on are keys to virtually all spheres of life.

Professors who are loved and respected by students bring out the best in their pupils. Military leaders who "walk the talk" in the heat of battle command the loyalty and trust of subordinates for a lifetime. It is no different in the business or sporting arenas. The executive or coach with a reputation for putting the team first will, over time, always trump the leader who is suspected of aiming for personal glory.

In one of the most important and (once you hear it) obvious insights into human relationships ever made, the fourth-century BC Greek philosopher Aristotle, star pupil of Plato, said that all of us tend to believe the views of people we already trust. The point is deceptively simple and bears constant reflection on the part of leaders. Aristotle rightly observes that even a brilliantly argued case from someone we dislike or whose motives we think dubious will fail to carry the same force as the case put forward by someone we regard as transparently good and trustworthy. I will say much more about this in chapter 8. For now I just want to emphasize that life "example" is essential to leadership.

The Heart of Leadership

These four tools of leaders — ability, authority, persuasion and example — are not, as I have already hinted, of equal importance. The leader who relies on ability and authority without due emphasis on persuasion and example is likely to be regarded as something of a despot. It leads to a kind of tyranny and to widespread disillusionment as the team begins to suspect that every decision is about the leader, not the organization. Brigadier Wallace warns against a form of leadership that cannot, or will not, suppress ego: "then people quickly realise it's about us, and any natural advantage fades and leadership becomes hard work."[8]

What about the leader who relies on persuasion without life example? Quite simply, he will not be able to sustain people in a vision. The team might believe for a while, but it will grow cynical. "He's all talk," they'll say. As I write, I keep hearing just this sort of commentary from conservatives when they discuss Obama. As an outsider, I cannot judge, but it illustrates the danger of having excessive skills of persuasion — or, at least, of relying on those skills excessively — and not concentrating on matching rhetoric with concrete action. Conversely, the executive who relies on life example without a clear-cut leadership ability to persuade others will be well-loved, but she won't be able to lift people beyond themselves to aspire toward a goal. Leadership is not about popularity. It is about gaining people's trust and moving them forward.

As I said earlier, I can't help feeling that *authority* is the least useful tool of leadership. *Ability*, of course, remains necessary; leaders rarely emerge from the pack without some talent. No doubt it is obvious that I consider *persuasion* and *example* (in combination) to be the heart of leadership. To put it bluntly, people can be effective leaders with little structural authority and a modicum of flair, but they are unlikely to lead well without significant doses of persuasion and example.

Again, this is because leadership is fundamentally relational: effective communication and building trust are key aspects of all relationships, whether in marriages, families, political movements or multinational corporations. The "*human* side of management," as Thomas Teal of the Boston Consulting Group calls it, is all-pervasive but sometimes overlooked. Leaders must be fully cognizant of the fact that their role "is not a series of mechanical tasks but a set of human interactions."[9] If that is so, nothing can be more important to leadership than persuasion and example.

When you think about it, some of most influential leaders in history got by without structural authority through their immense power of persuasion and life example. I am thinking of epoch-changing people like Jesus of Nazareth, who was a Galilean peasant brutally executed by Roman might

Copyright © Kanu Gandhi/GandhiServe

Gandhi presenting a birthday present to Nandini his secretary's niece, August 1944.

and yet who somehow reset the Western calendar and reshaped Western culture. From the East think of Mahatma Gandhi, a mid-level lawyer with little actual political power, even as the head of the Indian National Congress. But his vision of an India free of hatred (and British rule) and his austere protest-fasts and practices of nonviolence made him the most influential man in the subcontinent during the 1920s and 1930s and the "father of the nation" for modern Indians. The London-based *Hibbert Journal* of 1918 predicted with accuracy the rising influence of Gandhi:

> Persons in power should be very careful how they deal with a man who cares nothing for sensual pleasure, nothing for riches, nothing for comfort or praise, or promotion, but is simply determined to do what he believes to be right. He is a dangerous and uncomfortable enemy, because his body which you can always conquer gives you so little purchase upon his soul.[10]

Similar things could be said about Elizabeth Cady Stanton's nineteenth-century fight for woman's suffrage, Martin Luther King's civil rights movement, Nelson Mandela's opposition to apartheid, and Desmond Tutu's Truth and Reconciliation Commission.

Of course, all of this may sound rather rarified and unattainable. Few of us are destined to be epoch-changers. Nevertheless, the point deserves reflection: massive influence can be exerted with minimal structural authority as long as maximal persuasion and life example exist.

More to the point, I imagine many readers will be able to personalize the point. Think of the people who have had the most influence in your life over the years. Did they achieve that influence through their structural power over you? I doubt it. I have already mentioned my Year 5 school teacher, Henry Bingham. Yes, he was my teacher, so in that sense he had authority, but I distinctly remember him as one of the least domineering personalities in the school. Yet, he was able to calm me down in the explosions of anger that occasionally followed my father's death in a plane crash, and he was able, through the force of his gentle trustworthiness, to guide me away from some of the sillier decisions that a hyperactive eleven-year-old can make.

Through my teenage years the biggest influence on my life was not my football coach, who could kick me off the team, or my Kung Fu master, who could kick my butt, but a middle-aged volunteer at the school who taught "Scripture" once a week. In Australia one relic of Christendom is a one-hour lesson about religion in government schools. It is serviced by volunteers, not teachers (which made it infinitely more attractive than officially supervised "non-Scripture"). The Scripture-teaching women — they were usually elderly women — had no authority, and so it was often a free-for-all.

At fifteen I had no intention of attending church or of taking religion seriously. My upbringing was loving but completely god-*less*. My Scripture teacher had the courage one day to invite the class for discussions at her home on Friday afternoons. She promised hamburgers, milkshakes and scones. A group of us took her up on the offer, thinking that a few minutes of God-talk was a small price to pay for free and copious food. In that lounge room on those Friday afternoons were the class clown and bully, a petty thief, drug users and sellers and various other kinds of happy pagans. She showed us quite extravagant patience and hospitality, put up with having her video cassette recorder stolen one week and even housed one of our totally inebriated mates for a night in her beautiful suburban mansion following a drunken Year 10 party around the corner. This is not the book for Damascus Road conversions and, frankly, my perspective on faith is not as simple and straightforward as it was in my late teens, but the influence of Mrs. Weldon on the direction of my life is lasting. It was an influence totally without authority, full of persuasion and example.

I could offer other examples from academic life or from the corporate sphere. But I'm sure these suffice to underline what many readers already know from their own experience: whether it is Mahatma Gandhi transforming one of the largest countries on earth or the mentor who saved us from rookie errors early on in our career, leadership is fundamentally about relationships and so requires, first and foremost, the relational instruments of persuasion and example.

The point of this discussion about the nature and tools of leadership is not to offer anything groundbreaking or controversial but simply to explain why I place such a premium on the virtues, and especially on the virtue of humility, for the leader's task. Let me offer a simple syllogism that the rest of the book will, I trust, demonstrate:

a. Persuasion and example are keys to effective leadership.
b. Humility enhances persuasiveness, partly because it is a compelling character trait in leaders.
c. Therefore, humility is important for leadership.

Practicing humility has the potential to enrich a leader's effectiveness. I hope by the end of this book, you will be convinced of the logic, beauty and benefits of humility. Let me start with the logic.

CHAPTER 3

Common Sense

The Logic
of Humility

BEFORE DISCUSSING THE ORIGINS AND OUTLINING some practical benefits of humility, I want to offer a simple, logical argument for cultivating the virtue in both personal relationships and professional dealings. *Humility is common sense.*

None of us is an expert at everything. I know that statement is obvious, but it is worth letting its significance sink in. Despite the collective brilliance represented by my readers, what we don't know and can't do far exceeds what we do know and can do. A little humility, then, is hardly rocket science. It is common sense.

Some may have heard the less-than-true story of four people on a plane that lost all power in the engines and started careering toward the ground. The pilot announced the problem and added, "There are four of us but only three parachutes. It's my plane, my parachutes—I have to take one of them." The others agreed. He strapped the parachute on and jumped to safety. Left on the aircraft were a brilliant professor (a rocket scientist, no less), a minister of religion and a backpacker. The professor jumped to his feet insisting, "I am one of the greatest minds in the country. I must survive. I must take one of the remaining parachutes." The others agreed. He prepared himself and launched out.

The elderly clergyman started to explain to the young traveler, "I've lived a long life. I do not fear death. You take the last parachute." She stopped him mid-sentence with, "No, it's fine. That brilliant professor just jumped out with my backpack strapped on!"

Though untrue, the story illustrates something that is undeniably true. Expertise in one area counts for little in another. That is a particular problem jumping out of a plane with nothing but a PhD and a backpack. But it is equally troublesome here on the ground. Knowing a great deal in one area of life is no guarantee of proficiency in another, despite the fact that some of us engage in what you might call competency extrapolation.

Competency Extrapolation

I will never forget an awkward conversation with a renowned engineer and family friend about Dan Brown's *The Da Vinci Code*. I mentioned over lunch that historians found the novel's premise quite funny—my own ancient history department was running seminars at the time humorously debunking its more outrageous claims. My friend wouldn't have a bar of it. It was substantially true, he insisted, and nothing I said changed his mind, even though he knew my doctoral work was in the relevant field.

I was observing competency extrapolation. Because his judgment about things mechanical was so astute and widely sought after, he backed himself on matters far outside his specialty. We all do this sometimes. I hate to think how often my friends have put up with my unconsciously projecting confidence in historical matters about which I know little (I sometimes fear this book is a case in point). There is a danger in knowing a lot. As the ancient Greek proverb warns: "Knowledge puffs up, but love builds up."[1]

True experts ought to be more conscious of their limitations than most. Knowing a lot in one area should, in theory, underline just how much there is to know outside your specialty. I could discuss the Roman sacking of Jerusalem in AD 70 until all my readers were asleep: we would start with a chapter on General Pompey's entry into Palestine in 63 BC, move onto one about the crushed rebellion in Sephoris in 4 BC, then the increased tax impositions of AD 6, the growing agitations of freedom fighters in the 40s, the murderous activities of the *sicarri* or "dagger men" in the 60s, and finally, the all-out war of AD 66–70, climaxing in the bloody four-month siege of Jerusalem, in which countless fleeing residents were crucified by the surrounding Roman legions until, as one ancient source puts it, "so great was their number, that space could not be found for the crosses nor crosses for the bodies."[2]

But knowing a fair bit about obscure events of ancient history ought to remind me instantly of how much there is to know in the numerous fields I have never studied — other periods in history, let alone science, mathematics, business, politics, education, sport and medicine. Knowing a lot *in fact* demonstrates how much I don't know. Expertise could legitimately be described as uncovering the depths of my ignorance. It is a principle that leaders should ponder regularly.

Take Mandy, the newly-appointed CEO of an IT firm. She had previously been a hotshot senior manager in a fast-growing telco, so her move to the computer software industry seemed "doable", to herself and others. But she soon learned that a talent for seeing the big picture and a flair for motivating teams will take you only so far. Within a year she was feeling out of her depth. Telecommunications is not IT. There were industry subtleties she had overlooked and technical information she had failed to study. If she were able to have her time over again, she would execute the transition with more grace and a listening ear.

In particular, Mandy would have sat down more with Serena, the unassuming middle manager who had been with the company fifteen years. More than once this woman saved Mandy from a public gaff with her gentle passing comments and advice. Serena was one of those incredible people whom CEOs easily overlook. She probably has the knowledge and skill to ascend the corporate heights but decided long ago that she was perfectly happy working a forty-five-hour week and getting $80,000 per year. How else could she have raised three girls, chaired the local Parent-Teacher Association for nearly a decade and taught herself to speak fluent French.

Or take Santino, a biology teacher elevated five years ago from Head of the science department to school Principal. Everyone applauded the appointment at the time because his leadership had made the school a "centre for excellence" in science and technology. The expectation was that he could do the same for the other departments. It soon became apparent that what worked for science did not work for other subjects. The successful science open days he had conducted, where the public could view rat dissections, chemistry experiments and laser shows, proved nontransferable for liberal arts subjects, despite Santino's best efforts.

He soon realized he had been guilty of competency extrapolation and quickly called a meeting with the heads of the English, drama and art departments. He apologized for the mistake—a difficult thing to do before the condescending English Head—and asked them to devise their own plans for profile-raising relevant to their respective fields. The core idea was the same—public engagement—but the execution had to be radically different. "I've always wanted to hold an art show," said the near-retirement art teacher, "but we would need a significant prize to make it work." On the spot Santino offered $3,000, unsure where in the budget he would find the money but determined to give it a go. The show has just completed its third year with well over two hundred entrants from the surrounding schools and wider community. It now pays for itself and already there are small signs of rejuvenation and increased enrolment in the art department.

Stories like these are mere illustrations of the central idea of this chapter: none of us is an expert at everything, so a little humility is common sense. Humbly acknowledging limitations and refusing to engage in competency extrapolation are not signs of weakness. They demonstrate realism and are therefore strengths. The opposite, in fact, is a serious weakness and a complete unreality. A story is told — apparently it is true — of Muhammad Ali during the peak of his career. I understand that he is now a truly humble man and that many of his public antics were just showmanship. But on one occasion as he was flying interstate to defend his world heavyweight title the captain abruptly announced, "Approaching severe turbulence. Would passengers and crew fasten seatbelts immediately?"

Heavyweight boxer Muhammad Ali during a news conference he conducted from inside the ring in Atlanta, Ga., Oct. 24, 1970.

Normally, *some* turbulence means severe turbulence, so I hate to think what was in store. The crew hurried up and down the aisles to check that everyone was safe before strapping themselves in. One flight attendant noticed Muhammad Ali toward the front of the aircraft with a seatbelt obviously resting on his lap, undone. "Excuse me, sir. Would you please fasten your seatbelt?" she asked. "The captain has advised this could be quite rough."

Ali looked at her and calmly said, "Superman don't need no seatbelt."

Quick as a flash she replied, "Superman don't need no *plane*!" I would love to have seen the world champ's face in that moment. He loved wit, and I can only imagine he secretly admired this feisty attendant. In any case, there is a jarring unreality 30,000 feet in the air in the middle of a storm daring to think you do not need the seatbelt, when in fact you need not only the belt but the crew, the pilot *and the plane*.

Self-Deception

Muhammad Ali offers a rather over-the-top example, but this should not obscure the fact that some of us, especially the clever, skilled or gifted, sometimes fool ourselves (and occasionally others) into thinking we are supermen and superwomen in our circles of influence. But usually this is self-deception, and it is a perennial problem for people with healthy egos and large imaginations, which happens to be most leaders. In his superbly titled *I Told Me So*, philosophy professor Gregg Elshof explores the ubiquitous nature of self-deception in public and private life, in secular and religious communities. It is one of the most disturbingly insightful books I have read, and from the opening page it made me squirm:

> A mother somehow manages not to notice the obvious signs that her son is on drugs. A wife does the same with respect to her husband's affair. All of the evidence is easily available. Yet it goes unseen. The young man puts out of mind the horrors of the sex-slave industry driving the pornography business and convinces himself that these women actually enjoy their work. The politician convinces himself that his lofty ends justify morally ambiguous means (or worse). The director of a Christian non-profit organization manages to find sincerely compelling a perspective from which money donated to the ministry can legitimately be used to pay for an extravagant personal vacation or, perhaps, a private jet. This book is about self-deception. It's about the amazing human capacity to break free from the constraints of rationality when truth ceases to be the primary goal of inquiry.[3]

More relevant to the present chapter is the research Elshof cites from Thomas Gilovich, professor of psychology at Cornell University. A survey of one million high school seniors found that 70 percent of them thought they were "above average in leadership ability". Only 2 percent thought they were "below average". In terms of "ability to get along with others", *all* students thought they were "above average", 60 percent thought they were in the "top 10 percent" and 25 percent thought they were "in the top 1 percent". It might be tempting for us adults to explain this as the arrogance of youth or the extravagance of the Y-Generation (that in itself would be a self-deception strategy). But the Gilovich research also found that 94 percent of college professors think they, too, are doing a "better-than-average job".[4] It is a fact of our nature, it seems, that most of us have a grossly exaggerated sense of our own abilities.

Whatever our skills and expertise, what we don't know and can't do far exceeds what we do know and can do. Despite the power of self-deception—and, indeed, as its antidote—a good dose of humility is common sense.

The Universe

So far, my contention that humility is common sense has involved what you might call a *horizontal* argument. When we compare ourselves to others, especially to the entire community of others, our skills, gifts and knowledge base, however great, have only relative significance. Our personal competencies are well worth celebrating but not extrapolating without restraint.

There is also a *vertical* argument for humility. When we look "up" at the universe, most of us rightly feel spookily small. I know this is not the usual Management 101 kind of talk, but neither is it without significance for the rounded leader. This is one of those difficult subjects to talk about in public. I sometimes have to tread a fine line when speaking on this theme to mixed audiences in corporations or educational institutions. If I use the word "God", my atheist friends get upset and accuse me of proselytizing or being insensitive to their convictions. If I deliberately avoid "God" and go for the more nebulous "universe", our Jewish, Christian, Muslim, Hindu, Sikh and nameless God-fearing buddies feel I am deliberately excluding the majority viewpoint to pander to a minority of atheists (still less than 10 percent in most western countries).[5]

My compromise language, then—which is likely to please no one—is "Mind". My defense is that this is the same language used by some of the world's great physicists, from Michael Faraday in the nineteenth century to Albert Einstein in the twentieth to Paul Davies and others in the twenty-first century (none of whom could be described either as religious believers or atheists).[6] The universe we observe has all the hallmarks of an immense "mind". Its incredible complexity combined with its mathematical elegance causes those who comprehend such things to speak of their wonder and awe. Apparently, the quasi-religious sensation many of us experience watching a magnificent sunset or standing before Niagara Falls can be felt through an understanding of the beautiful formulae regulating everything from the movement of the planets to the behaviour of DNA.

Ferdinand Schmutzer, 1921

Albert Einstein during a lecture in Vienna in 1921

The incomparable Albert Einstein, whose theories of special and general relativity changed our view of the universe forever, was, as I say, neither a religious believer nor an atheist. In an interview of 1954, the year before he died, Einstein was asked his views on "God". He replied, "I do not believe in the God of theology who rewards good and punishes evil. My God created laws that take care of that. His universe is not ruled by wishful thinking, but by immutable laws."[7] In a letter two years earlier he noted how his understanding of the "harmony" of nature *humbled* him. He contrasted this with what he perceived to be the typical attitude of the "free-thinkers" (a once-common label for atheists):

> I am also not a "free-thinker" in the usual sense of the word because I find that this is in the main an attitude nourished exclusively by an opposition against naive superstition. My feeling is insofar religious as I am imbued with the consciousness of the insufficiency of the human mind to understand deeply the harmony of the Universe which we try to formulate as "laws of nature". It is this consciousness and humility I miss in the Free-thinker mentality.[8]

This perfectly states my point: the mysterious harmony of the laws of nature should lead thinking people—whether believer or otherwise—to an attitude not far off humility.

Adding to this sense of marvel before nature is the intriguing discovery in recent decades of the "fine-tuning" of the universe. Apparently, from the nanosecond after the beginning of the cosmos, matter strangely obeyed certain "rules" that were absolutely necessary for the formation of stars, carbon and, therefore, life as we know it. I am no expert on these things — my historical knowledge goes back a blink-of-an-eye by comparison — but one important text on the subject (*Universes* by Professor John Leslie, a specialist in the philosophy of science and a nonreligious man) summarizes these rules or "physical constants" as follows:

> *Rate of expansion*. The cosmos threatened to recollapse within a fraction of a second or else to expand so fast that galaxy formation would be impossible. To avoid these disasters its rate of expansion at early instants needed to be fine tuned to perhaps one part in 10^{55} (which is 10 followed by 54 zeros …).
>
> *Weak nuclear force*. Had the nuclear weak force been appreciably stronger then the Big Bang would have burned all hydrogen to helium. There could then be neither water nor long-lived stable stars. Making it appreciably weaker would again have destroyed the hydrogen: the neutrons formed at early times would not have decayed into protons.
>
> *Strong nuclear force*. For carbon to be created in quantity inside stars the nuclear strong force must be to within perhaps as little as 1 per cent neither stronger nor weaker than it is.
>
> *Electromagnetic force*. With electromagnetism very slightly stronger, stellar luminescence would fall sharply. Main sequence stars would then all of them be red stars: stars probably too cold to encourage Life's evolution and at any rate unable to explode as the supernovae one needs for creating elements heavier than iron. Were it very slightly *weaker* then all main sequence stars would be very hot and short-lived blue stars.[9]

Leslie's introduction to the "fine-tuning" features of the universe is five pages long, and the chapter on this topic runs to thirty pages. But you get the idea. We live in a universe that looks uncannily as if it was expecting us. In his superb *A Short History of Nearly Everything* Bill Bryson says of fine-tuning, "What is extraordinary from our point of view is how well it turned out for us."[10] The same point has recently been made by one of the preeminent biologists of our time, Simon Conway Morris, professor of evolutionary palaeobiology at the University of Cambridge (UK). In *Life's Solution* he writes:

> Whether it be by navigation across the hyperdimensional vastness of protein space, the journey to a genetic code of almost eerie efficiency, or the more familiar examples of superb adaption, life has an extraordinary propensity for its metaphorical hand to fit the glove ... As with the audacious and intelligent Polynesians [who could navigate vast oceans with pinpoint accuracy], so life shows a kind of homing instinct.[11]

Please be clear about my point. In talking about these cosmic mechanics I am not trying to explain away the mystery of creation or slip in a soft argument for belief in divinity. My practical point concerns humility. Whether the universe was majestically designed by Someone or is the result of a glorious, imponderable Coincidence, believer and atheist alike can agree that we are infinitesimally small in this vast universe *and* infinitely blessed or lucky to be here. We can all stand in awe of the amazing fact that we find ourselves living in a universe that not only operates according to elegant "laws", but has somehow, through those laws, produced a world of sentient beings *who can now comprehend those laws*. The fact that there are "laws" is odd; the fact that our brains comprehend those laws is spooky. Influential British philosopher John Macmurray puts his finger on this mystery:

> Why should the world not have been structured with infinite delicacy, but in a mode which passed our comprehension and of which we had no means even to be aware? How does it come about that at times the scientist, by purely theoretical calculation can define in advance an unknown aspect of the order of nature which is then looked for and found? And all these ways of thinking, such as mathematical calculation, have their origin, and their primary uses, in the service of our human purposes. They are devices we have elaborated as a means to our ends. Is it not something of a miracle, then, that they should turn out to be means to a comprehension of the orderly structure of the world?[12]

Whatever you call it — intention or luck — the nature of the universe and the fact that our minds understand that nature are uncanny in the extreme and should result in something close to humility. Renowned atheist Richard Dawkins quotes with approval fellow atheist Michael Shermer's sense of wonder at nature:

> What can be more soul shaking than peering through a 100-inch telescope at a distant galaxy, holding a 100-million-year-old fossil or a 500,000-year-old stone tool in one's hand, standing before the immense chasm of space and time that is the Grand Canyon, or listening to a

scientist who gazed upon the face of the universe's creation and did not blink? That is deep and sacred science.[13]

Perhaps at this point I should admit to a niggling doubt about the viewpoint of Dawkins, Shermer and others—and my atheist friends have never really given me a satisfying answer. How can atheism guarantee the *dignity of humanity*, which is needed in a proper definition of humility? Believers and atheists alike can feel small and overawed before a majestic universe, but feeling small is not the same as being humble. Humility, as I said in the first chapter, assumes the inherent dignity of the one being humble—it is a lowering of oneself from a height. Atheism certainly promotes a low view of humanity—how much lower can you get than thinking yourself an accidental by-product of a series of even larger accidents!

But how can the atheist at the same time logically argue for humanity's inherent worth (beyond the ten dollars of minerals that make up the body)? Of course, this isn't a problem for most of us; the vast majority believes in some kind of Creator who *intended* us, and where there is intention or purpose there is dignity. Atheists, however, reject all such purpose. "There is at the bottom: no design, no purpose, no evil, and no good," writes Prof Dawkins, "nothing but blind, pitiless indifference. DNA neither knows, nor cares. DNA just is, and we dance to its music."[14] Even allowing for a little rhetorical exaggeration here, this is a pretty low view of existence.

Perhaps conscious of this implication, Dawkins has more recently insisted that atheism in fact increases one's view of life's value: "the knowledge that we have only one life should make it all the more precious. The atheist view is correspondingly life-affirming and life-enhancing."[15] This is surely a non sequitur. Having only *one* life enhances its preciousness only if existence is inherently valuable in the first place. The sandstone pebble in my garden doesn't become precious just because it's the only one there. A gold nugget, on the other hand, is a different story.

Please don't misunderstand me. Not for a second am I suggesting that atheists cannot or do not act with humility toward others. I am simply pointing out, as an aside, that atheism lacks the *theoretical framework* for the kind of humility described in this book. Humility involves both a sense of finitude and a sense of inherent dignity.

In any case, I hope the larger point remains. Whichever way you look at it, whether *horizontally* in relation to the human family or *vertically* in relation to the majestic wonder of the universe, there is a certain logic to keeping pride in check and conducting ourselves, regardless of our various competencies, with humility toward others. Thoughtful people recognize that what they don't know and can't do far exceeds what they do know and can do. And in their more pensive moments, they pause to acknowledge with wonder their tiny but blessed (or, if we insist, *lucky*) place in the vast universe. Humility, in other words, is common sense.

CHAPTER 4

Aesthetics

How the Humble
Are Beautiful

THE CLASSICAL GREEK TERM FOR "VIRTUE" IS
aretē. Someone's *aretē* was their "excellence", whether some
bodily splendor, physical prowess or ethical beauty. A virtuous person was *attractive*, worthy of praise. The Greeks
probably took this idea too far: it was common for them to
expect public honour for their "virtues". Nevertheless, there
is a truth contained in the word *aretē* that is worth recover-
ing. There is an *aesthetic* dimension to virtue. In real life,
as opposed to in celluloid, we are attracted to the good and
repelled by the bad. Even the woman who says she prefers
the archetypal "bad boy" probably doesn't actually like it
when he is bad toward her.

In business, sport, the military or anywhere you care to
mention, we are more attracted to the great who are humble
than to the great who know it and want everyone else to
know it as well. It is a simple psychological reality for most
in our culture that humility (rightly understood) is regarded

as beautiful. In chapter 1 I told the story of Joe Louis, the professional fighter who refused to respond to the insults of the young men, withheld his power for their good and was happy for them to learn who he was only after the incident. A story like this increases our estimation of the man. That's the aesthetics of virtue. In the remainder of this chapter I want to underline this point with some striking historical and contemporary examples.

Sir Edmund Hillary

In 1953 Sir Edmund Hillary conquered Mount Everest with his Sherpa friend and guide, Tenzin Norgay. What they achieved, especially with the kind of equipment available at the time, stands as one of modern time's truly great physical feats. Hillary was duly honoured. Later in 1953 he was knighted; in 1985 he was made New Zealand's high commissioner to India, Nepal and Bangladesh, and in 1995 he received the British realm's highest award, the Order of the Garter (membership of which is limited to just twenty-four individuals). More important to Hillary were his efforts to give back to the Nepalese something of what they had given him. Through the Himalayan Trust, established in 1960, he built hospitals, airfields and schools. He epitomized *the noble choice to forgo status, deploy resources and use influence for the good of others before himself.*

One story captures the essence of Sir Edmund Hillary's outlook. On one of his many trips back to the Himalayas he was spotted by a group of tourist climbers. They begged

New Zealand's Sir Edmund Hillary in Jan. 20, 2007.

for a photo with the great man, and Hillary obliged. They handed him an ice pick so he would look the part and set up for the photograph. Just then another climber passed the group and, not recognizing the man at the centre, strode up to Hillary saying, "Excuse me, that's not how you hold an ice pick. Let me show you." Everyone stood around in amazed silence as Hillary thanked the man, let him adjust the pick, and happily went on with the photograph.

It doesn't matter how experienced that other climber was; his greatness was diminished by this intrusive presumption. We are repelled by pride. Edmund Hillary's greatness, however, is somehow enhanced by this humility. When I tell you this story your estimation of him increases, especially as we know that this individual episode was typical of his entire approach to life: forgoing status and resources for others. The *Encyclopædia Britannica*, not normally given to heaping praise on the subjects of its entries, declares: "Hillary never anticipated the acclaim that would follow the historic ascent ... Throughout [his life] ... he maintained a high level of humility, and his main interest came to be the welfare of the Himalayan peoples of Nepal, especially the Sherpas."[1] Humility is beautiful.

Albert Schweitzer

Albert Schweitzer (1875 – 1965) was a supremely gifted philosopher, historian and biblical scholar, as well as being a highly accomplished musician. He wrote what many regard as the twentieth-century's most important academic book on the life of Christ, *The Quest of the Historical Jesus*; he also wrote a masterpiece on the music of Johann Sebastian Bach for good measure and is described as "the foremost authority of his time on the composer".[2] To the shock of many, at the height of his career he left academia, completed a medical degree and devoted himself to medical work in Gabon, West Africa, becoming known throughout the world as the "jungle surgeon". He won the 1952 Nobel Peace Prize and, true to form, gave the prize money to a leper hospital. In his autobiography, *Out of My Life and Thought*, he tried to explain his life

AP Images

German-born Dr. Albert Schweitzer, 80-year-old biblical scholar, musician, philosopher, writer and physician, October 17, 1955.

choices to some who thought him crazy and to others who hailed him a hero:

> Only a person who feels his preference to be a matter of course, not something out of the ordinary, and who has no thought of heroism but only of a duty undertaken with sober enthusiasm, is capable of becoming the sort of spiritual pioneer the world needs. There are not heroes of action—only heroes of renunciation and suffering. Of these there are plenty. But few of them are known, and even they not to the crowd, but to the few … Those who are given the chance to embark on a life of independent action must accept their good fortune in a spirit of humility. They must often think of those who, though equally willing and capable, were not in a position to do the same.[3]

Daniel and Janet Matthews

As Schweitzer says, some heroes of "independent action" are unsung. My favourite Australian example is virtually unknown outside of obscure historical circles. Only three generations ago Aboriginal people in Australia were being shot for bounty, raped at leisure, and filled with alcohol for the fun of the spectacle. It was widely believed in Australian society that Aborigines were less than human. Based on quasi-evolutionary assumptions, many settlers considered the indigenous people to be a "throw back" to our ape ancestry and therefore devoid of a "soul".

But there were some beautiful exceptions. Daniel Matthews lived with his wife, Janet, on the Murray River in

Mr Maloga: Daniel Matthews and his Mission, Murray River, 1864-1902. University of Queensland Press, Brisbane, 1976

Janet Matthews

Victoria from the 1860s through to the turn of the century.[4] They ran the successful "Matthews Brothers Central Merchants", providing food, clothing and other vital supplies to the settlers up and down the river. They also owned a large plot of land just out of town. By the standards of the time the Matthews lived a reasonably comfortable (albeit hard-working) life.

Things soon changed, however. Matthews's journal records the moment he witnessed a large number of Aborigines in a desperate, poverty-stricken and drunken state. That night he wrote words that would begin an amazing journey for him and his family, "My God! Can this be right?" From that day, the Matthews committed themselves to the service of the Murray River Aboriginal people. Daniel would use his resources for the good of others before himself.

Daniel Matthews had a way with words, and he used it powerfully as an advocate for the Aboriginal people. It is reported that he systematically wrote to every newspaper and government agency in the country, begging the Australian leaders and public to change their attitudes toward the indigenous people. Mostly his words fell on deaf ears, but he has left us with some of the most lucid and moving pieces of writing about Aborigines in our nation's history.

Early on he discovered that his property had previously been regarded by the local indigenous people as sacred land (known to them as "Maloga"). His response was to give a large portion of it back to them. From that day, Maloga Station (as it became known throughout Austra-

Daniel Matthews

Mr Maloga: Daniel Matthews and his Mission, Murray River, 1864-1902. University of Queensland Press, Brisbane, 1976

lia) was to be used for the Murray River people, not for the Matthews' commercial profit. Maloga became a safe haven for Aborigines all over New South Wales and Victoria. The locals could freely hunt and fish there. They received medical attention (disease in the mid-1800s was rampant) and a European education for those who wanted it (Janet was a school teacher), and, when the fish were low, they were assured of a meal.

It was common in this period for lone settlers to chain a young Aboriginal girl to his bed—to be used at leisure. When Daniel heard that this happening in his area, he daringly marched into the settler's house, broke the chains or ropes and rescued the girl. On more than one occasion he was shot at and beaten up.

Despite the pleading of his brother William to concentrate more on the shop and less on Maloga, Daniel could not pull himself away. Matthews Bros., previously a thriving business, went broke. From what we can piece together of his life, Daniel Matthews worked an eighteen-hour day, six days a week, for almost four decades. And it took its toll— on his business, his health, his family and his friendships. Many of his contemporaries thought he was crazy, often saying, "He's got black-fellas on the brain."

The friendship and affection the Aborigines felt toward Daniel Matthews is epitomized in the title they bestowed on him, "Maranooka" (a special word for "friend"). It captured so much of the relationship between Matthews and the indigenous people of New South Wales and Victoria. In 1887 a journalist from the *Footscray Advertiser* was sent from Melbourne to write a story on Maloga station. The article concludes with some insightful words about Matthews's extraordinary willingness to hold his power for the good of others above himself:

> The superintendent (Matthews), I gather from outside sources, has impoverished himself and his family, being forced to neglect his own material interests through his extra care and affection for the blacks. I left the place feeling that a life had been given away in devotion to the natives' welfare.[5]

Whatever the journalist's perspective, the Matthews family did not feel they had thrown their life away. They believed they were holding their power and resources for the good of those who needed them most. Daniel died in 1902, but Janet, whom he had long described as the reason he had been able to fight so long and so hard, continued the work for another decade after her husband's death, even opening another two "missions" near Mannum in South Australia. The mark they both left on the Aboriginal people of Victoria, South Australia and New South Wales was deep and long lasting. Daniel Matthews's grave, which I visited some years ago in a kind of personal pilgrimage, has a modest tombstone and an inscription that reads: "Maranooka (Friend). His works do follow him."

Galileo and Newton

Galileo Galelei (1564–1642) and Isaac Newton (1642–1727) are two of the greatest scientists ever to have lived, but they seemed to approach their work with quite different outlooks. Galileo's significance can hardly be overstated. He, "perhaps more than any other single person,"

Justus Sustermans, 1636

Portrait of Galileo Galilei by Justus Sustermans painted in 1636.

wrote Stephen Hawking recently, "was responsible for the birth of modern science."[6] His demonstration of the Copernican view that the earth *in fact* revolved around the sun, contrary to contemporary scientific and religious doctrine, and his studies of the laws of motion were gargantuan feats of imagination, observation and mathematics.

77

Galileo seems to have known of his own greatness and enjoyed flaunting it at the expense of others. His arrogance has sometimes been overstated, and it is always difficult to psychoanalyze people from another era, but the great astronomer was known to refuse to collaborate with his contemporaries, most notably Johannes Kepler, who was considered one of the greatest astronomers of Europe. He dismissed out of hand Kepler's research, including his (correct) supposition that the planets orbited the sun in an elliptical rather than circular movement, and he described Kepler's assertion that the moon caused the tides as a fiction.

When Kepler, who greatly admired Galileo, wrote to him seeking his opinion of his discoveries, Galileo proved a poor and arrogant correspondent, once taking twelve years to reply to one of Kepler's letters. In a moment of unrestrained, and I hope rare, egomania Galileo wrote in his 1623 tract *The Assayer* (written in the form of a letter to a colleague): "You cannot help it, Signor Sarsi, that it was granted to me alone to discover all the new phenomena in the sky and nothing to anybody else. This is the truth which neither malice nor envy can suppress."[7]

Contrast all this with Sir Isaac Newton, born the year Galileo died. Newton has also been called the Father of Science, and his work on gravity, motion and classical mechanics, to name just a few, changed the scientific landscape. His legacy remains (with a necessary recasting of his ideas in light of the discoveries of Einstein). Despite these extraordinary achievements, Newton was a famously humble man, acknowledging that he had been aided by the

Engraving of Sir Isaac Newton by William Thomas Fry in mid-19th century.

Library of Congress, LC-USZ62-95738

work of other men and that science was a collaborative process.

In a letter to Robert Hooke in 1675 Newton wrote: "If I have seen further, it is because I am standing on the shoulders of Giants." The expression "standing on the shoulders of Giants" was not original to Newton, but its use by one of the world's greatest intellects is a salient reminder. On another occasion he described himself as "a boy playing on the seashore", searching for interesting shells and pebbles "while the great ocean of truth lay all undiscovered before me." Here was a man willing to admit that what he did not know far exceeded what he did.

No doubt, these two historical portraits of equally great men elicit different responses. Most of us, on hearing of Galileo's spiteful pride toward others, feel his greatness is somehow diminished. Conversely, the quotes from Newton enhance our appreciation of him. Humility makes the great even greater.

Unfortunately, in reading about Newton my own admiration for him took a dive when I came across a story of his own spiteful unwillingness to share glory with another. In his most famous work, *Mathematical Principles of Natural*

Philosophy (published 1687), often described as the foundation of modern physics, he had relied on important data about planetary movements provided to him by John Flamsteed, the Astronomer Royal at Greenwich Observatory. However, later the two men were involved in a decade-long spat. Newton, now President of the Royal Society, forcefully insisted that Flamsteed make other celestial data available for his use. Flamsteed refused. Newton responded by systematically removing all references to the Astronomer Royal in future editions of his *Mathematical Principles of Natural Philosophy.* How is this the same man who had earlier declared, "If I have seen further, it is because I am standing on the shoulders of Giants"?

I suspect you are now experiencing some of my disappointment with Newton. If greatness is enhanced by humility, it is doubly diminished by pride and false humility. My point here is not to make a judgment about Galileo or Newton, of course, but to underline the central theme of this chapter. There is an undeniable aesthetic dimension to virtue. We are naturally attracted to the good and equally repulsed by the bad. When humility is sincere — when words are matched by behaviour — it is indeed beautiful. Fortunately, the example of Sir Edmund Hillary remains untarnished.

Beautiful CEOs

There is no doubt that humility is attractive in the corporate world too. It is striking to read the comments of employees in the firms Jim Collins studied. In a section titled "Compelling Modesty", he quotes Nucor board member Jim Hlavacek describing the company's CEO Ken Everson:

> Ken is a very modest and humble man. I've never known a person as successful in doing what he's done that's as modest. And, I work for a lot of CEOs of large companies. And that's true of his private life as well. The simplicity of him. I mean the little things like he always gets his dogs at the local pound. He has a simple house that he's lived in for ages.[8]

Other notable CEOs in the study include Darwin Smith, who, despite taking Kimberly-Clark's cumulative stock returns to 4.1 times the general market over his twenty-year leadership, later reflected on his tenure in the words: "I never stopped trying to become qualified for the job."[9] "We found leaders of this type," remarks Collins, "at the helm of every good-to-great company during the transition era."[10]

Collins concludes the chapter on "Level 5 Leadership" with a personal reflection revealing his own admiration for the CEOs he had closely studied:

> All of us who worked on the finding have been deeply affected and inspired by the idea ... [These leaders] have become models for us, something worthy to aspire toward ... For like all basic truths about what is best in human beings, when we catch a glimpse of that truth, we know that our lives and all that we touch will be the better for the effort.[11]

Unlike Collins, I cannot bring myself to quote some of the counterexamples from the study. And there are some doozies! Needless to say, arrogance is as ugly as humility is beautiful.

The point of this chapter is not to advise us all to "put on" humility in order to impress our friends and colleagues. That would be a rather perverse inversion of the concept I am advocating. For now I am happy for us simply to notice the beauty of *humilitas* (and corresponding ugliness of arrogance) and to allow that reflection to begin its own work in us. Humility is not an ornament to be worn; it is an ideal that will transform.

CHAPTER 5

Philotimia

Why the Ancient World Didn't Like Humility

So far I have been talking as though humility were *universally* admired, as if the aesthetics of virtue, *aretē*, have always and everywhere been attached to the practice of forging status and deploying resources for others before yourself. They haven't. And the ancient Greeks are a case in point. I hope I am not overloading readers with pretentious ancient words—*humilitas* and *aretē*—but here's another worth knowing: *philotimia*. The ancient Greeks *loved honour*. The *Oxford Classical Dictionary* explains:

> *Philotimia*, literally the love of honour (*timē*). The pursuit of honour(s), tangible or intangible, was a constant of elite behaviour throughout Graeco-Roman antiquity; all that changed was its context and the extent to which it was given unbridled expression or else harnessed to the needs of the community at large.[1]

Honour and Shame

One of the most difficult things for ancient history students to get their heads around when first exploring the subject is the place Mediterranean societies gave to *honour* and *shame*. Honour was universally regarded as the ultimate asset for human beings, and shame the ultimate deficit — so much so that academics frequently refer to Egyptian, Greek and Roman societies simply as "honour-shame cultures". Much of life revolved around ensuring you and your family received public honour and avoided public shame.

Uppermost in a father's mind in the ancient world was not whether his son would be happy (in the modern sense) or make money or live morally, but whether the boy would bring honour to the family, especially to his father, and to himself. This might be accomplished through participation in a military victory, advancement through the ranks of official society or by some great service to the village. In all of these things the thought was not so much the importance of conquering evildoers, making a difference to civic life or benefiting others; the chief good was the respect and praise that comes through these activities and the way they confirm the merit of the one so honoured.

This is not to say ancient people did not value justice, social order and kindness — they certainly did. I am just saying that the honour one gains through such things was considered a high and noble goal. The flipside was that among a person's greatest fears was to be publicly shamed. To offer a blunt example that doesn't involve too much exaggeration, a Roman husband whose wife was found to be having an affair would feel more injured by the public shame she brought on him than by the betrayal of love itself. Ancient husbands could be as jealous as anyone in the modern world, but shame was the greater catastrophe.

All of this might be hard for moderns to understand. That is because most of us no longer live in honour-shame societies. Our key axis points are things like good-evil, pleasure-suffering and prosperity-poverty. Honour and shame still have some value for us—who doesn't crave a bit of praise and avoid public embarrassment?—but few of us would regard these things as the defining parameters of human life.

By contrast, without denying the importance of goodness, pleasure and prosperity, most ancient Greeks and Romans would not have thought about such things as the goals of human endeavour. Aristotle's third-century BC dictum seemed to them eminently sensible: "Honour and reputation are among the pleasantest things, through each person's imagining that he has the qualities of an important person; and all the more so when others say so."[2]

Aristotle goes on to explain his terms: "Good reputation is a matter of achieving the respect of all people, or of having something of the sort that all or the general public or the good or the prudent desire." And what is honour?

> Honor is a sign of a reputation for doing good, and benefactors, above all, are justly honored, although one with the potential of doing good is also honored ... The components of honor are sacrifices made for the benefactor after death,

memorial inscriptions in verse or prose, receipt of special awards, grants of land, front seats at festivals, burial at the public expense, statues, free food in the state dining room … [and on the list goes].[3]

It probably won't surprise you to learn that in a society that placed such a high value on honour, humility was rarely, if ever, considered virtuous. In the 147 pithy maxims of the *Delphic Canon* (6th century BC), considered by ancient Greeks to be the sum and substance of the ethical life, there is no mention of the theme of, let alone the word, "humility". The range of moral advice found in the *Delphic Canon* is impressive:

- "Control yourself."
- "Help your friends."
- "Practise prudence."
- "Return a favour."
- "Nothing to excess."
- "Act on knowledge."
- "Honour good people."
- "Don't curse your sons."
- "Rule your wife."
- "Mete out justice."
- "Despise no one."
- "Worship divinity."
- "Don't mock the dead."
- "Don't let your reputation go."
- "Respect the elder."
- "Respect yourself."

- "Die for your country."
- "Don't trust fortune."

The list goes on, but "humility" is conspicuous by its absence.[4] I cannot imagine a contemporary list of even *ten* virtues, let alone 147, that did not mention humility.

As I said in chapter 1, the word *humilitas* and its Greek equivalent *tapeinos* usually carried the negative meaning of "being put low". It was an undignified inability or refusal to establish your merit. Aristotle again provides insight into the ancient mind. In discussing situations that calm people down—as opposed to agitate conflict—he refers to the "humble" person, not at all meaning the gracious, other-person-centred character we are exploring, but rather, the weak and insipid man who poses no threat:

> People are also calm toward those who humble themselves toward them and do not contradict them; for they seem to admit being inferiors, and inferiors are afraid, and no one who is afraid belittles. That anger ceases toward those who humble themselves is evident even in the case of dogs, who do not bite those sitting down.[5]

Humility before the gods, of course, was appropriate, because they could kill you. Humility was advisable before the emperors too, for the same reason. But humility before an equal or a lesser was morally suspect. It upset the assumed equation: merit demanded honour, thus honour was the proof of merit. Avoiding honour implied a diminishment of merit. It was shameful.

None of this is to say that people could not be honourable

and modest in the ancient world. Sometimes we hear stories of great people who gladly gave up status. Lucius Quinctius Cincinnatus, for example, was a fifth-century BC Roman aristocrat who, during a civil emergency, was "called from the plough" to become dictator of Rome in 458 BC. He promptly assembled an army, defeated the rival Aequi tribe and then happily returned to his farm to resume normal life. Quinctius was an example in Roman tradition of two highly prized ideals: austerity, the shunning of luxury and willingness to live a disciplined life; and modesty, the opposite of hubris.

"The story was frequently cited as a moral example," explains Tim Cornell in the *Oxford Classical Dictionary*, "illustrating the austere modesty of early Rome and its leaders."[6] The Romans distinguished between *modestia* and *humilitas*. The former was a dignified restraint, the latter a shameful lowering. You can be sure old Quinctius was never described as possessing *humilitas*. He, like other Greeks and Romans, prized honour above virtually everything else.

Boasting

It was in this context that ancient Greeks and Romans thought nothing of praising themselves in public or, better still, getting others to praise them. No one appreciated crass boasting or boasting that put others down—hubris or arrogance. Nor was self-love advisable, as the Greek myth of Narcissus falling in love with his reflection teaches. But taking hold of the honour due to your merit was perfectly acceptable.

© Marie-Lan Nguyen/Wikimedia Commons

Marble bust of Emperor Augustus at the British Museum (c. 14 AD).

It was taken for granted that those with merit would seek the honour due to them. This was *philotimia*.

Perhaps the most famous expression of love-of-honour is the *Res Gestae Divi Augusti*, *The Achievements of the Divine Augustus*, written by the emperor Augustus himself (63 BC–AD 14) and, by his order, inscribed on bronze tablets to be set up in front of his mausoleum. Copies were distributed throughout the empire. It is one of the most important sources from ancient times, providing not only a catalogue of the emperor's activities (which we can check against other texts and archaeological remains), but also a rare glimpse into a mind-set that valued public honour above virtually everything else.

When you remember that this account (just 2,500 words in the original Latin) was penned by the emperor himself in the first person, you realize how little cringe there was in the period over self-congratulation and how different the ancient and modern worlds are in this respect. The emperor takes us through his thirty-five key areas of accomplishment topic by topic—military victories, public awards, gifts to the city at his own expense, building projects, civic games and so on. Here is a taste:

1. At the age of nineteen on my own responsibility and at my own expense I raised an army, with which I successfully championed the liberty of the republic when it was oppressed by the tyranny of a faction. On that account the senate passed decrees in my honour enrolling me in its order in the consulship of Gaius Pansa and Aulus Hirtius ...

10. My name was inserted in the hymn of the Salii by a decree of the senate, and it was enacted by law that my person should be inviolable for ever and that I should hold the tribunician power for the duration of my life ...

12. In accordance with the will of the senate some of the praetors and tribunes of the plebs with the consul Quintus Lucretius and the leading men were sent to Campania to meet me, and honour that up to the present day has been decreed to no one besides myself ...

15. To each member of the Roman plebs I paid under my father's will 300

Wikimedia Commons

A portion of the text of the Res gestae Divi Augusti, the self-celebratory autobiography written by emperor Augustus.

sesterces [at least two month's wages], and in my own name I gave them 400 each from the booty of war in my fifth consulship, and once again in my tenth consulship I paid out 400 sesterces as a largesse to each man from my own patrimony, and in my eleventh consulship I bought grain with my own money and distributed twelve rations apiece, and in the twelfth year of my tribunician power I gave every man 400 sesterces for the third time. These largesses of mine never reached fewer than 250,000 persons . . .

22. I gave three gladiatorial games in my own name and five in that of my sons or grandsons; at these games some 10,000 men took part in combat. Twice in my own name and a third time in that of my grandson I presented to the people displays by athletes summoned from all parts . . .

25. I made the sea peaceful and freed it of pirates. In that war I captured about 30,000 slaves who had escaped from their masters and taken up arms against the republic, and I handed them over to their masters for punishment . . .

34. In my sixth and seventh consulships, after I had extinguished civil wars, and at a time when with universal consent I was in complete control of affairs, I transferred the republic from my power to the dominion of the senate and people of Rome. For this service of mine I was named "Augustus" by decree of the senate, and the door-posts of my house were publicly wreathed with bay leaves and a civic crown was fixed over my door and a golden shield was set in the Curia Julia, which, as attested by the inscription thereon, was given me by the senate and people of Rome on account of my courage, clemency, justice and piety. After this time I excelled all in influence.[7]

The Life and Works of Flavius Josephus, William Whiston, John C. Winston Company; Philadelphia, Toronto, 1957 edition

Engraving of Flavius Josephus by J. Rogers.

Self-congratulation was not just the special interest of emperors. Ordinary citizens of limited significance felt at liberty to parade their best accomplishments before others. Take the famous autobiography of Josephus, a military commander, turncoat and chronicler of the Jewish people, who fortuitously predicted the ascension of Vespasian (from general to emperor) and then lived out his years in Rome under imperial patronage. The opening words of the book (an *auto*biography, remember) will strike modern readers as bizarre, but they would not have raised an eyebrow in first-century Roman circles:

> My family is not an ignoble one, tracing its descent far back to priestly ancestors. Different races base their claim to nobility on various grounds; with us a connection with the priesthood is the hallmark of an illustrious line. Not only, however, were my ancestors priests, but they belong to the first of the twenty-four courses — a peculiar distinction — and to the most eminent of its constituent clans. Moreover, on my mother's side I am of royal blood ... [he lays out the details]
>
> With such a pedigree, which I cite as I find it recorded in the public registers, I can take leave of the would-be

detractors of my family. Distinguished as he was by his noble birth, my father Matthias was even more esteemed for his upright character, being among the most notable men in Jerusalem, our greatest city. Brought up with Matthias, my own brother by both parents, I made great progress in my education, gaining a reputation for an excellent memory and understanding. While still a mere boy, about fourteen years old, I won universal applause for my love of literature; insomuch that the chief priests and the leading men of the city used constantly to come to me for precise information on some particular in our ordinances.[8]

Josephus goes on but you get the idea. Nowadays, we would be horrified if someone, however great, opened their autobiography with such obvious self-aggrandizing. But this was perfectly normal in antiquity. As long as these things were true—which they probably were in the case of Josephus—the merit warranted the praise, even if it was self-praise. In these paragraphs, as in the *Res Gestae*, we catch a glimpse of one of the profound cultural differences between ancient Mediterranean society and the modern Western world. And the difference came about not through a slow evolution of ethical reflection but through a kind of humility revolution.

CHAPTER 6

Cruciform

How a Jew from Nazareth Redefined Greatness

So, what happened? How did the culture move from being one that prized public honour and despised lowering yourself before an equal (let alone a lesser) to one that despises self-aggrandizement and prizes lowering yourself for others. Whence humility?

I mentioned in the introduction that I was involved in a research project at Macquarie University's Department of Ancient History exploring the origins of humility as a social virtue. This is what prompted my friend's quip about my "objective distance from the subject". I won't burden you with the technicalities of the findings but the conclusion was clear: the modern Western fondness for humility almost certainly derives from the peculiar impact on Europe of the Judeo-Christian worldview. This is not a "religious" conclusion; Macquarie is a public university with no division of theology or even religious studies. It is a purely historical finding.

God of the Underdog

Ancient Israel, no less than ancient Greece, was an honour-shame society. Humility before God was appropriate, of course, as was humility before judges, kings and priests, but lowering yourself before an equal or lesser in early biblical times would not have seemed fitting.[1] Something changed, however, in the later biblical period. As Israel struggled under foreign domination—and sometimes under local oppression—the prophets began to speak of the Almighty's special concern for the crushed and humiliated. The word used of such people is "humble" or "humbled".[2] Here, the typically negative meaning of the term—to be put low—is used positively in the way we might talk about "the poor" or "the oppressed". Negative words are employed sympathetically. This may well have been the first step in the journey toward "humility", as we understand it.

Perhaps reflecting on the Maker's soft spot for the downtrodden, one text from the second century BC urges humility toward both the great and the lowly. The Jerusalem sage Yeshua Ben Sira told his students: "Humble your head before the great. Incline your ear to the poor and return their greeting in humility."[3] The first line is to be expected: everyone knew you should be lowly before the great. The final expression is striking and may be the first attempt in history to use the word "humility" to describe how ordinary people should treat equals (or, in this case, a social inferior).

There is some indication that ancient people found this a weird concept. When Ben Sira's original Hebrew text was translated into Greek around 132 BC, the translator (Ben Sira's grandson) changed the word "humility" in this passage to "gentleness", a much more acceptable term for Greeks.[4] He was happy to say *Humble* your head before the great" — everyone thought that was smart — but not "return the poor's greeting *in humility*." Whatever Ben Sira originally meant by a "humble greeting", his grandson thought it best to soften the meaning. We are still a long way, then, from the "humility revolution" that occurred less than two hundred years later. And it would be another Jewish teacher who sounded the call.

The Teacher from Nazareth

Unfortunately, after two thousand years of Christian history it is difficult for people in the modern West to think of Jesus of Nazareth in a non-theological way. The mere mention of his name arouses either spiritual devotion or social awkwardness. Try saying at a dinner party, "I recently read something interesting about Jesus" and just watch the reaction. Your Christian buddies will rejoice and think you've seen the light, and your sceptical friends will probably change the subject lest the interest become contagious. Interestingly, you probably would not get the same response if you opened with, "I've been reading about Aristotle" or "Julius Casear" or even "a teacher called Ben Sira". You might sound pretentious but not weird.

But historians approach the figure of Jesus no differently from Aristotle, Caesar or Ben Sira. This thought might trouble Christian readers and puzzle the religiously sceptical. It is just a simple fact of the academy in state universities all over the world that Jesus remains a figure of historical interest. Scholars do not privilege the writings about him (the New Testament and few scraps of non-Christian evidence), but neither do they dismiss them out of hand just because they happen to be talk about the man who founded what eventually became the largest religion in the world.

Frankly, even I — who have both a historical and personal interest in the man — can forget about theology and religion when teaching about Jesus' life in a university setting. I hope I don't lose my Christian readership at this point, but in the eighteen hours of lectures I deliver each year on "the historical Jesus", I find it possible not to think of him as "my personal Lord and Saviour". I simply lay out the sources for his life, describe the methods historians use for testing claims about him, place him in the context of Roman and Jewish history and outline what most scholars, regardless of their religious convictions, agree are the facts about Jesus' life, teaching, execution and immediate impact. I could just as easily be discussing "the historical Julius".

It's in this context that I want to outline the impact that Jesus of Nazareth had on the Western notion of humility. Whatever hints we find in pre-Christian Mediterranean literature about the need for a little humility some of the time toward some people are eclipsed by the full-blown call

Wikimedia Commons

Mosaic of Christ washing the feet of Saint Peter from the Nea Moni monastery, Greece.

for humility found in the writings that would shape Western civilization.

Perhaps surprisingly, explicit teaching about humility does not feature strongly in the record of Jesus' sayings. Of course, we get humble-sounding statements like, "Blessed are the poor in spirit, for theirs is the kingdom of heaven," "Blessed are the meek, for they will inherit the earth," "Love your enemies," and the famous "If someone strikes you on the right cheek, turn to him the other also."[5] But only once do you get an explicit statement:

> Take my yoke upon you and learn from me, for I am gentle and humble in heart, and you will find rest for your souls. For my yoke is easy and my burden is light.[6]

"Yoke" is a common way of referring to a rabbi's system of teaching, and here the teacher's *gentleness* and *humility* are offered as reasons for embracing his teaching. Jesus is not saying, "Hey, accept me because I'm such a humble guy!" He is contrasting his own "light" approach to the ethical life with the burdensome rules demanded by rival teachers of the period — many of whom advocated the memorization and practice of literally thousands of commandments concerning work, rest, eating, hand-washing, sex, farming, prayer, study and so on. The reference to himself as "humble" is hardly a boast in a period when humility still had an ambiguous meaning. The word principally meant *lowliness* or *submissiveness*. Humility was the stuff of slaves, not respected rabbis.

On another occasion Jesus seems to have delighted in turning upside-down ancient notions of greatness and servitude:

> Whoever wants to become great among you must be your servant, and whoever wants to be first must be slave of all. For even the Son of Man [his favourite way of referring to himself] did not come to be served, but to serve, and to give his life as a ransom for many.[7]

Here, Jesus as good as says that true greatness consists in self-sacrifice—his impending martyrdom being the prime example. Please be clear. We are still in the realm of history. Despite quotations from Jesus and references to his death, this is not theology; still less is it an attempt to promote one religion over another. We are simply tracking where the modern notion of humility as a positive ethical virtue came from. And there is little doubt that the Jew Jesus had something to do with it. This chapter and the previous one bear out the observation of British social philosopher John Macmurray that "three old civilizations have been mixed together to form the culture of which we are the heirs—the Hebrew, the Greek and the Roman."[8]

A Cruciform Culture

Interestingly, what established humility as a virtue in Western culture was not Jesus' persona exactly, or even his teaching, but rather his *execution*—or, more correctly, his followers' attempt to come to grips with his execution.

Unfortunately, two thousand years of religious art, architecture and Christian kitsch have domesticated the image of a cross, stripping it of its historical shock and awe. Crucifixion was the ancient world's *summum supplicium* ("ultimate punishment"). It was reserved for political rebels and slaves. Of the three official methods of capital punishment—crucifixion, decapitation and burning alive—crucifixion was regarded as the most shameful and most brutal. Victims were usually scourged with a leather strap embedded with metal and pottery, stripped naked, led out to a public place and nailed (or tied) to a large wooden beam, where they could expect to endure hours, sometimes days, of excruciating pain and eventual asphyxiation. The Roman philosopher Seneca (4 BC–AD 65), the leading intellectual of mid-first-century Rome, morbidly reflects on this most shameful of deaths:

Lucius Annaeus Seneca, sculpture by Puerta de Almodóvar in Córdoba.

Wikimedia Commons

Can anyone be found who would prefer wasting away in pain, dying limb by limb, or letting out his life drop by drop, rather than expiring once for all? Can any man be found willing to be fastened to the accursed tree, long sickly, already deformed, swelling with ugly tumours on chest and shoulders, and draw the breath of life amid long-drawn-out-agony? I think he would have many excuses for dying before mounting the cross![9]

This is the death that the followers of Jesus saw their master face. The greatest man they had ever known was brought down to the lowest place the Roman world could envisage: death by crucifixion.

Jesus' death has, of course, been the subject of enormous theological reflection, the most important being the affirmation that he died as an atoning sacrifice for the salvation of the world. But this is not our concern here. More important for the current discussion is the way the first followers of Jesus began to rethink the entire honour-shame paradigm in which they had been raised. As I have already said, ancient Mediterranean cultures pursued honour and avoided shame at all costs. Honour was proof of merit, shame the proof of worthlessness. But what does this say about the crucified Jesus? That was the question confronting the early Christians. Logically, they had just two options. Either Jesus was not as great as they had first thought, his crucifixion being evidence of his insignificance, or the notion of "greatness" itself had to be redefined to fit with the fact of his seemingly shameful end.

Opponents of early Christianity happily accepted the first option. The crucifixion was incontrovertible evidence that Jesus was a pretender to greatness. Powerful testimony to this point of view—the dominant perspective for at least two hundred years after Jesus—has been discovered scratched into a guardhouse wall on Palatine Hill in Rome. Archaeologists uncovered a piece of anti-Christian graffiti dating back to the second or third century, when large numbers of Christians were still being imprisoned and executed. The crude drawing (about 50 cm by 30cm) shows a crucified man with a donkey's head, indicating stupidity. Next to the cross stands a man with arm raised in adoration toward the figure on the cross, and below the image scribbled in very bad Greek are the words, "Alexamenos worships his god." The most plausible explanation of the graffito imagines Roman guards taking perverse pleasure in deriding an incarcerated Christian named Alexamenos by depicting his "Lord" as a mule-headed loser. In an honour-shame culture what else could Jesus' crucifixion have meant?

akg-images

Christians took the other option. For them the crucifixion was not evidence of Jesus' humiliation (*humilitas*) but proof that greatness can express itself in humility (*humilitas*), the noble choice to lower yourself for the sake of others.

"Alexamenos worships his God" (2nd or 3rd century AD).

The first datable reference to this innovation in ethical reasoning comes from a letter written by the apostle Paul to the Christians in the Roman colony of Philippi in northern Greece. The letter is dated to about the year 60, almost exactly the same time as Seneca penned his morbid account of crucifixion quoted above. The contrast is astonishing. In the quotation that follows Paul urges his readers to live in humility, choosing to think of others as better than themselves. He then drives the point home by quoting a hymn, presumably one known and sung in Philippi, that speaks of Jesus' *humilitas* on the cross:

> Do nothing out of selfish ambition or vain conceit, but in humility consider others better than yourselves. Each of you should look not only to your own interests, but also to the interests of others.
>
> Your attitude should be the same as that of Christ Jesus [then comes the hymn]:

Who, being in very nature God,
    did not consider equality with God something to be
        grasped,
but made himself nothing,
    taking the very nature of a servant,
    being made in human likeness.
And being found in appearance as a man,
    he humbled himself
    and became obedient to death
        —even death on a cross![10]

Believe it or not, these few words are the subject of literally hundreds of scholarly books and articles. Of most interest to biblical historians is the clear reference to Jesus as "in very nature God". Somehow the first followers of Jesus went from thinking of him as a teacher and prophet to singing hymns to him as God incarnate. And this happened in just three decades—within living memory of the addressees of this letter.[11]

But just as astonishing as the early description of Jesus as "God" is the fact that these first Christians could in the same breath say (or sing) "God" and "cross". The idea that any great individual, let alone the Almighty, could be associated with a shameful Roman crucifixion is just bizarre. Contemporary Christians may find the thought easy enough, but that's only because of two thousand years reflection on this narrative. Western history is now utterly "cruciform"—shaped by the event of Jesus' crucifixion.

What we read in the above text is nothing less than a humility revolution. Honour and shame are turned on their heads. The highly honoured Jesus lowered himself to a shameful cross and, yet, in so doing became not an object of scorn but one of praise and emulation. As Paul says in his introduction to the hymn, "In humility consider others better than yourselves ... Your attitude should be the same as that of Christ." Honour has been redefined, greatness recast. If the greatest man we have ever known chose to forgo his status for the good of others, reasoned the early Christians, greatness must consist in humble service. The shameful place is now a place of honour, the low point is the high point.

A curious sign of this strange reversal of thinking is found in Sir Edmund Hillary's decision to mark his achievement by leaving a small crucifix on the summit of Everest. I don't know why Hillary did this; he wasn't an overtly religious man. Perhaps it was a token of his own humility, trying to honour a "higher power" at the moment of his own triumph. Then again, maybe it was just the one symbol of Western civilization that he could fit into his small pack. In any case, it is worth noting that what to the ancient mind would have seemed a perverse symbol of accomplishment, to the modern mind makes perfect sense: of course you would put a cross at the highest point of the world!

Within decades of Paul's letter to the Philippians Christians were regularly emphasizing "humility" as a central characteristic of the ethical life. The New Testament provides evidence of this,[12] but to offer an example from just a few decades after the biblical period, a letter from a Roman church official named Clement (AD 96) to the Christians in Corinth says: "You are all humble-minded, not boastful, yielding rather than domineering, happily giving rather than receiving."[13] By now humility is firmly established as *aretē*, a virtue, within Christian circles. It took a couple of centuries for this to catch on throughout the Roman/Western world, but once it did, it became commonplace for people, whether or not they were Christians, to use the once negative words *humilitas* and the Greek equivalent *tapeinos* in the positive sense of deliberately lowering yourself for the good of others—namely, humility.

A Christian Monopoly on Humility?

Let me head off a potential misunderstanding of the argument in this chapter. Not for one moment am I suggesting that Christians have a monopoly on humility. Everyone knows that believers and unbelievers alike are capable of spectacular arrogance and wonderful humility. Sadly, although the Judeo-Christian framework is responsible for the Western world's fondness for this virtue, the church itself has been guilty of hubris and bigotry at many points in its history.

This is not just a Roman Catholic problem, with their Crusades and Inquisitions; Protestants, too, have had their fair share of shameful departures from Christ's example. Martin Luther, the German founder of the Protestant movement, wrote the most spiteful and supercilious things about European Jews in his 1543 tract *The Jews and Their Lies*. The chief of the Reformed tradition, John Calvin, a theological hero for me, was anything but humble in his treatment of heretics like Michael Servetus, whom he had executed in 1553 for deviant views on the Trinity.

I find it difficult to understand how the one who said, "Whoever wants to become great among you must be your servant,"[14] has been represented at times by men with an entirely different notion of power and greatness. Then the historian in me pipes up and asks: Isn't it possible there are things in my own life and culture that later generations will (rightly) find despicable? I'm sure it is.

My point is not that Christians alone can be humble; rather, as a plain historical statement, humility came to be valued in Western culture as a consequence of Christianity's dismantling of the all-pervasive honour-shame paradigm of the ancient world. Today, it doesn't matter what your religious views are—Christian, atheist, Jedi Knight—if you were raised in the West, you are likely to think that honour-seeking is morally questionable and lowering yourself for the good of others is ethically beautiful. That is the influence of a story whose impact can be felt regardless of whether its details are believed—a story about greatness that willingly went to a cross.

Put another way, while we certainly don't need to follow Christ to appreciate humility or to be humble, it is unlikely that any of us would aspire to this virtue were it not for the historical impact of his crucifixion on art, literature, ethics, law and philosophy. Our culture remains cruciform long after it stopped being Christian.

CHAPTER 7

Growth

Why Humility
Generates Abilities

IT'S TIME TO TALK ABOUT SOME PRACTICAL BENEFITS
of humility. Sure, it's logical, beautiful and has an interesting history, but what does it do? How does it help? At one
level, this question may seem out of place: surely, virtue is
its own reward and humility should be practised for its own
sake, not for the sake of some material or social outcome.
John Macmurray, former professor of moral philosophy
at the University of Edinburgh and one of the twentieth-
century's leading social thinkers, would disagree. He had a
somewhat stormy relationship with the Christianity of his
youth, but in a book titled *The Clue to History* he wrote of
his fascination with Jesus' statement, "Blessed are the meek,
for they shall inherit the earth":[1]

> Our tendency is to treat this as an assertion that humility
> is one of the supreme virtues ... A sermon on this text is
> almost inevitably a sermon on the virtue of humility. I find
> it difficult to imagine it as a sermon on how to inherit the

earth. Indeed it is more likely to lead to a general injunction against the desire to be successful in the material field, and so to become a panegyric on those who turn from an interest in this world to a purely "spiritual" conception of goodness. It is this kind of treatment of the teaching of Jesus that gives point to the communist contention that religion is "opium for the people" and that it is used to persuade the poor and unfortunate classes to be content with their lot. Yet it is quite obvious that Jesus gave as his reason for believing in humility that it was an essential part of the means to ultimate material success. Nothing could be less characteristic of the mind of Jesus than the notion that virtue is its own reward.[2]

I'm not sure I agree with everything Macmurray says here, but I am convinced of his central point, evident everywhere in his writings: virtue is not an ethereal preparation for "otherworldly" existence; it is practical engagement in the here-and-now and has untold social implications *and benefits* for those who walk in its path.

The Slow Pace of Pride

Perhaps the most obvious outcome of being humble is that you will learn, grow and thrive in a way the proud have no hope of doing. The logic is simple: people who imagine that they know most of what is important to know are hermetically sealed from learning new things and receiving constructive criticism. I see this at conferences all the time, whether in business, education or not-for-profit settings. Every conference seems to have a Proud Peter. He's the guy in your organization who is moderately talented and charming but whose years in the business have created an inflexibility when it comes to learning from others or implementing changes. His natural wit is able to point out the smallest difficulty with a new idea, and so he quickly convinces himself and sometimes others that the old way — his way — is probably best.

Perhaps it's just my imagination, but I think I can often spot the Proud Peters when I address various audiences. He typically sits up the back with arms folded or behind his head, and throughout the talk he offers quips to his buddies, who politely smile. He never takes notes — that would be too keen — but he is frequently the first to raise a hand during the Q&A. He might damn the speaker with faint praise or else pose a question designed to sound clever. Afterward in the staff debriefing I imagine he resists adopting any fresh insights. He is closed to new thoughts (that aren't his own) and rarely submits himself to review or criticism. His pride impedes his progress.

"Arrogant managers," writes J. P. Kotter of the Harvard Business School, "can overevaluate their current performance and competitive position, listen poorly, and learn slowly."[3] If my account sounds uncannily accurate, it's because "Proud Peter" is my unfortunate natural tendency. I frequently catch myself at conferences — when I'm not the speaker — thinking of quips and devising critiques. I also sit up the back!

Then there is Humble Heather. She is no less competent than Peter, and no less self-confident. But she has a keen awareness that what she doesn't know and can't do far exceeds what she does know and can do. She has an attractive mix of steely will and intellectual gentleness. She is not as popular as Peter, but she has more friends. People trust her, respect her and open up to her. And because she is not at all intimidating, despite enjoying relatively senior status in the organization, colleagues feel free to question her. Over the years she has learnt never to resent this. Some of her best ideas came in a flash of insight after someone queried the wisdom of her first suggestion.

At conferences Heather sits neither up the back nor at the front. She's happy to go wherever her friends are. She takes notes. Heather follows the lecture so intently that the speaker uses her as a gauge of how well the material is going over. She smiles, frowns, concentrates and laughs. She whispers to those around her but only, I imagine, to confirm what's just been said with some anecdote from her own experience. She is just as likely as Peter to ask a public question, but her tone is different. She might look for clarification about something she didn't understand or just wonder out loud how the material applies to her specific situation. Her motivation is to arrive at the truth, and she usually gets there. Her humility—deciding to "consider others better" than herself—often leads to new knowledge and methods.

Coincidentally, as I was writing this book, I was drifting off to sleep one evening when the BBC World Service carried a short piece on the origins of science—and humility featured prominently. Professor Raymond Tallis, a British medical scientist and philosopher, told the story of the invention of the clinical trial, a classic example of the scientific method applied to medicine; it was a classic example also of how humility fosters knowledge.

Tallis explained how an eighteenth-century ship's physician named James Lind had a hunch that scurvy was caused by the putrefaction of the body and could be remedied through the intake of acids. After much thought, Lind devised a clever test, subjecting his theory to the realities of nature. He took twelve sailors with scurvy and divided them into groups of two. In addition to normal rations, each group received various types of acidic supplements, cider, vinegar, oranges and lemons, and so on. After five days the "oranges and lemons group" had recovered. Lind didn't know exactly why it worked (we now know it was the Vitamin C), but he had empirical proof of the health benefits of citrus fruits.

Professor Tallis went on to describe the humility involved in Lind's novel approach to finding scientific truth: "the greatness of science consists not solely in moments of genius, but in the recognition that most apparent moments of genius are not." In other words, the wonderful thing about contemporary science is the way it subjects our best thoughts, our assumed moments of genius, to testing, to the possibility of being proved wrong. This was not easy for intellectual giants such as Lind, Newton, Galileo and others. It required "not only the conquest of the material world," Tallis observes, "but the conquest of human nature." It involved "not just knowledge of nature but a mature understanding of the limitations of our knowledge." In short, it demanded humility. Professor Tallis concluded his piece by saying as much: "So, let's hear it for James Lind.

The humility built into the very idea of the clinical trial: *I don't know whether this treatment based on anecdotal observation and consistent with my theories really works* is the opposite of the argument from authority."[4]

This *generating* effect of humility, whether in science or business, is beautifully described by the great literary critic G. K. Chesteron, in his cheeky book *Orthodoxy*. In his battle against early twentieth-century rationalism and self-reliance, which he believed was sapping the energy out of religion, the arts and life itself, Chesterton argued that human pride is in fact the engine of *mediocrity*. It fools us into believing that we have "arrived", that we are complete, that there is little else to learn. Humility, by contrast, he said, reminds us that we are small and incomplete and so urges us on toward the heights of artistic, scientific and societal endeavour:

> Even the haughty visions, the tall cities, and the toppling pinnacles are the creations of humility. Giants that tread down forests like grass are the creations of humility. Towers that vanish upwards above the loneliest star are the creations of humility. For towers are not tall unless we look up at them; and giants are not giants unless they are larger than we. All this gigantesque imagination, which is, perhaps, the mightiest of the pleasures of man, is at bottom entirely humble. It is impossible without humility to enjoy anything.[5]

Lessons from the Outback

Let me offer a personal, if trivial, example of how humility (of sorts) generates new knowledge and abilities. I used to sing in a band, back before I became a nerd. We toured the country playing in pubs and clubs, schools, universities, prisons and sometimes in Aboriginal communities in outback Australia. On one such occasion we were invited to perform for the indigenous community on the Daly River, two hundred kilometers southwest of Darwin in the top end of the country. As a sign of appreciation the locals took us out for a "bush tucker" lunch by a swamp in the crocodile playground that is the Daly. We were treated to a large goose, roasted water lily nuts and a large, oily turtle thrown onto the fire, ant-infested, still squirming.

As we sat in the dirt nervously looking over our shoulder at the water's edge, one of the elders asked if we wanted to

The author with his former band members learning the didgeridoo by the Daly River, Northern Territory, Australia, 1992.

learn to play the didgeridoo, the famous indigenous wind instrument used in sacred ceremonies and celebrations. We were musicians with a deep regard for Australia's Aboriginal heritage, so we lined up raring to go. I pushed myself forward to be the first. I was soon having second thoughts.

For the next five minutes this old fella spat down the hollowed hardwood log until saliva frothed over the top of the mouthpiece and dribbled out the end onto the dirt in front of me. At this point he passed it to me to play. "Put your lips on the mouth piece," he said without any indication this was all a crass joke played on visitors, "and just blow real slow and smooth." There I was sitting in the dirt by a crocodile swamp, about to eat half-cooked, ant-infested turtle, preparing to pucker up to the most saliva lubricated thing I had ever seen. I pressed my lips against the beeswax mouthpiece, took a deep breath (probably the wrong order of events) and blew. And I am so glad I did. Within a few weeks of this "lesson" I was playing fairly well. Soon we began to introduce the didgeridoo into some of our songs. The instrument became something of a signature sound for the band's live performances and it features in at least two of our albums.

I realize that telling you how I humbly sat in the dirt and picked up a new skill is not exactly humble. But I should clarify. This was forced *humilitas*. I didn't want to be there sitting in the dirt, eating turtle and sharing bodily fluids with my old Aboriginal friend. The moment was forced upon me. But I am glad for the lesson. Sometimes sitting in the dirt puckering up to the horrible is the place you learn skills you might not have picked up elsewhere. It is the confrontation at work where you decide to back down, the limitation you concede in front of others, the moment of scrutiny that finds you out. These humbling places are often the places of growth.

I am not talking about allowing others to walk all over you. That would be humiliation. Instead, I mean opening yourself up to the vulnerability of being wrong, receiving correction and asking others how they think you could do better. In this sense the low place is the high place. It is where you develop.

Undefended Leadership

Simon Walker teaches leadership at Oxford University in the UK. He speaks of the "undefended leader", the title of a trilogy of books he has written on the subject. He points out how frequently leaders feel the need to defend themselves publicly, whether in front of clients, executive peers or other staff. Leaders sometimes live in a hostile world, with young bucks ready to take their position at the first opportunity and stakeholders occasionally unforgiving of the smallest managerial mistake. Leaders thus imagine that appearing invincible and right is necessary for building loyalty and belief.

There are several strategies of defense. One is to *totally* separate the "frontstage" from the "backstage", to use Walker's image. In front of the team the leader appears forceful, focused, unfazed and decisive. Privately things are different.

"And then there is the leader's backstage life," says Walker, "in which he struggles with all his own unmet needs and unresolved problems. This is where all the frustration, the disappointment, the doubt, the failure, the weariness get pushed."[6] The point is not that the frontstage-backstage reality is bad; leaders have to keep many things from public view. It's just that the *overly* defensive leader will experience a disconnect between the public and private spheres. This can breed isolation and dishonesty and potentially lead to disproportionate outbursts of anger or frustration.

The undefended leader, however, while not "letting it all hang out", is honest with herself and allows trusted colleagues into the backstage rooms where they can offer timely feedback. The undefended leader moderates the pretense of total control and self-sufficiency and learns to receive from others just as much as she gives. In my language, she has learnt *humilitas.*

In his book *Leading Change* John P. Kotter explains how he tracked the careers of 115 of his former students from Harvard Business School. He tells the story of a Marcel, whom Kotter never really expected to show great leadership potential but who emerged as head of his own company and became very wealthy. At first Kotter wondered if the key was some "lucky break" that catapulted Marcel beyond his station. After discussion and reflection he ended up attributing Marcel's success to the way he gave humble attention to the difficulties and mistakes he endured through the years. "He reflected on good times and bad," writes Kotter, "and tried to learn from both. Confronting his mistakes, he minimized the arrogant attitudes that often accompany success. With a relatively humble view of himself, he watched more closely and listened more carefully than did most others."[7] Humility generates learning and growth.

Humility and Self-Esteem

There is a paradox worth observing in Walker's undefended leader, whom Kotter equally well describes as reflective, humble and careful to listen. Often those who are boastful, protective and unwilling to listen are actually the most insecure. It is a compensation mechanism, a way of hiding true feelings of inadequacy. After all, if I can make others think highly of me, then perhaps I am great after all. By contrast, the humble person, the one who doesn't feel the need to bignote herself, is the truly secure one. The logic is simple: if you have a robust view of yourself, you don't need others to affirm it, at least not as often.

Friends of mine have told me a true story about some friends of theirs, a husband and wife partnership, who own a posh jewelry store in Sydney. Some years ago an American gentleman walked in asking to buy a Pink Argyle diamond—one of the most expensive items in the shop. During the credit card transition the store's computer froze. The woman stared at the screen in embarrassment. The gentleman lent over the counter, offered a keystroke combination and the machine came back to life. "You know a little about computers, do you?" she said. He nodded, continued the transaction and quietly left the store.

When the woman's husband came into the shop later in the day, she told him about the sale and the embarrassment over the computer. When they looked again at the customer's credit card details, they were shocked to read: "Mr Bill Gates." True story! Gates happened to be in town for the huge Microsoft Convention at Sydney's Darling Harbour. The woman suddenly felt silly for having asked him, "You know a little about computers, do you?" when this is the guy who just about sets the agenda for the computer industry worldwide (except in the case of Mac users like myself).

Why didn't Gates advertise who he was when he offered his keystroke combination? It certainly would not have been his insecurity. Quite the opposite. I imagine—if it wasn't simply to avoid a fuss—Gates was just so comfortable in his shoes, so to speak, he felt no need to present himself as anything other than some anonymous American guy who "knew a little about computers". I don't know whether Bill Gates is a humble man. You hear mixed reports. My point is simply that, paradoxically, big-noters are often insecure and the humble are frequently secure.

AP Images

Bill Gates at a press conference in New York, June 26, 2006.

I'm no psychologist but I imagine that humility not only signals security; it probably fosters it too. I am increasingly convinced that a healthy self-worth is rooted far more in *service* than achievement, far more in *giving* than taking. For one thing, achievement is such a fragile basis for self-esteem. This is partly because high achievement is rare and difficult. It is also because the more you rely on achievement for a sense of worth, the more crushing every small failure will seem. It is analogous to the fashion model who depends on her beauty for a sense of personal value; every blemish is a disaster, and she lives with the reality that her beauty is sure to fade. Executives, sportswomen, high achievers of every kind, are setting themselves up for insecurity if they pin their sense of self-worth on their accomplishments.

One thing I know from undergraduate psychology and from years of counseling in a church context is that, in the end, nothing is more valuable to us, and value-adding, than good relationships. Knowing that we are loved and valued by those we love and value is *the* predictor of a healthy sense of self-worth. The teenage boy who sacrifices friendships while striving to become the star quarterback or centre forward is just setting himself up for insecurity. The CEO who only feels alive when her profit announcements make it into the paper is unlikely to feel comfortable in her own skin during a downturn.

By contrast, those who strive for the heights of achievement, while valuing relationships with family and friends above all else, will find their sense of worth maintained during the ups and downs of accomplishment. Relationships are where security is really found. And since humility—

holding your power for the good of others—can only enhance our relationships, I feel confident saying that humility not only signals security, it fosters it as well.

The Power of *Mea Culpa*

my fault

As I write, one of the world's most successful CEOs is facing the larger challenge of this chapter. Steve Jobs is the larger-than-life character at the centre of computer giant Apple. On 24 June 2010 Apple released the iPhone 4 to great fanfare. Within days it became clear there was an antenna problem—holding the device a particular way muffled the wireless signal and phone calls would drop out. It was dubbed the "death grip". People started to complain. Reviewers picked up on this and brought it to wide media attention. The company responded with press releases seeking to minimize the scale and importance of the problem. Criticism mounted.

Jobs then called a press conference at which he proclaimed, "We're not perfect." It was not quite the *mea culpa* we might have expected, especially since he added that "every phone has weak spots". Amazingly, he even started showing footage of competitors' devices—BlackBerry Bold and HTC Droid Eris—experiencing similar problems (later disputed by the manufacturers). In debating this might be called an "ad hominem diversion". It is rarely convincing.

Instead of copping it on the chin, apologizing to customers and learning from the lesson (the path of humility), Apple offered a makeshift solution. They sent unhappy consumers a free protective case for the phone. Industry analysts were unmoved, and the independent review magazine *Consumer Reports* announced it could not recommend the product—a first for Apple. A long-term fix is surely in the works, but the damage has been done. I have read more than one article in the mainstream press in the last few weeks accusing Apple's management of arrogance, a refusal to admit mistakes and an overreliance on the company's brand image to ride them out of the storm. But corporate image is a fickle thing, argues brand expert Allen Adamson of Landor Associates, who was quoted in

AP Images

Apple CEO Steve Jobs at the Apple iPhone 4 press conference at Apple headquarters in Cupertino, Calif., July 16, 2010.

the *Wall Street Journal* as saying, "If they (Apple) bury their heads in the sand, and don't engage in conversation and act in an arrogant way, they're going to erode a bit of their brand."[8]

I myself am a loyal Apple user—here I am writing on my Mac and researching newspaper articles on my iPad—but these events have slightly dented my esteem for the company and its leadership. The problem is not the technological glitch itself. It is how the company responded to criticism. There has been a resulting change in perception of Apple's corporate character. It is a fascinating truth worthy of every leader's reflection: mistakes of execution are rarely as damaging to an organization, whether corporate, ecclesiastical or academic, as a refusal to concede mistakes, apologize to those affected and redress the issue with generosity and haste.

Group arrogance (like personal arrogance) is offputting and stultifying, a point driven home forcefully by Jim Collins' follow-up to *Good to Great*, his 2009 book *How the Mighty Fall*. By contrast, humility is both attractive to the watching public and, importantly, the only ethos that will foster an organization's learning and development. Stephen R. Covey, the author of the bestselling *The Seven Habits of Highly Effective People*, writes in a more recent book:

> Humility truly is the mother of all virtues. It makes us a vessel, a vehicle, an agent instead of "the source" or the principal. It unleashes all other learning, all growth and process. With the humility that comes from being

principle-centered, we're empowered to learn from the past, have hope for the future, and act with confidence in the present.[9]

The humble place is the place of growth. Heather trumps Peter every time.

CHAPTER 8

Persuasion

How Character
Determines Influence

THERE IS PERHAPS SOMETHING ODD OR EVEN unseemly in writing a chapter on the way humility *influences* others. Isn't humility essentially about serving the interests of others? Why would you "use" humility to get your way with someone?

That's a fair question, and I have two responses. First, influence is not bad in itself. If I sincerely believe that an individual or organization is best served by moving in a new direction, influencing becomes an instrument of care. Parents influence their kids for their good. Close friends influence each other to protect them from potential mistakes. Military commanders influence their men in order to keep them out of harm's way. Second, whether or not we think that influencing others contradicts humility, it is a simple observational reality that the humble are frequently more persuasive and inspiring than the arrogant. It is just a weird reality, as I hope to show, that humility does influence.

How Leadership Works (Again)

Fundamental to influence is persuasion, and, as I argued in chapter 2, persuasion is at the core of leadership. I noted earlier that there are four tools of leadership. First is simple *ability*. Good leaders have nearly always excelled in some particular area before their move into general leadership. Football coaches were usually decent players in a former life. Business executives typically had success in one or another department of a firm. Senior pastors nearly always started kicking goals in youth work or pastoral care. Ability matters.

The second (and least useful) tool is structural *authority*, that is, the powers given to the leader by the organization — the power to hire and fire, the power to spend money, and so on. Since authority is not inherent but derived, good leaders know to use structural power sparingly.

The third and fourth tools of leadership I offered earlier are intimately related. *Example* is the leader's embodiment of integrity and authenticity. Without a life example that speaks louder than words, even the most persuasive leader will fail. People may be moved by insightful and well-crafted words, but they quickly lose confidence in the persuader if it becomes apparent that "She's all talk!" Finally, *persuasion* is the leader's ability to articulate and argue a position in a way that motivates others in the team to move in the new direction. A leader with example but with no ability to persuade others will be well loved but unable to lift people beyond the circumstances they can see around them. Persuasion is key.

The Textbook on Persuasion

But how does persuasion work? About three and a half centuries before Christ, the Greek philosopher Aristotle laid out a sophisticated theory about how we hear and assess arguments and so form our beliefs. His work *On Rhetoric* was the standard text on the topic of "persuasion" for two millennia, right up until it was decided that people could attend university without studying any Classics (a sad day). Long before our fascination with exposing media spin, long before Pulitzer Prize-winning journalist William Safire compiled his collection of *Great Speeches in History*,[1] readers of Aristotle looked to the ancient world's greatest mind to learn why some messages seem convincing to us and others do not.

According to Aristotle, arguments work — or don't work — because of three, interrelated factors: *logos*, the intellectual dimension; *pathos*, the emotional or personal dimension; and *ethos*, the social and ethical dimension of persuasion. For Aristotle *logos, pathos* and *ethos* are features of the persuader and her argument, but they are also factors within the audience. Take *logos*, the intellectual

Roman copy of bust of Aristotle after a Greek original from 330 BC, British Museum.

Marie-Lan Nguyen/Wikimedia Commons

aspect of persuasion. A speaker must have a cogent argument, well developed and rational in its form. But the speaker is also at the mercy of the audience's *logos*, their philosophical training, general intelligence and so on. A brilliant argument can fall on deaf ears if it offered to a thoughtless crowd. Mostly, though, Aristotle would say, audiences find themselves moved by logical argument, by *logos*.

While Aristotle was a master of formal logic, he was wise enough to know that *logos* alone was never enough to persuade people to adopt a significant, new viewpoint. We are not just intellectual beings, he insisted; we are also emotional and social beings, and these factors must be understood in the art of persuasion. Enter *pathos* and *ethos*. *Pathos* is the part of a message that appeals directly to our inner self, to our emotional and aesthetic needs. At the trivial level, *pathos* is a speaker's ability to move his audience with humour or tragedy or simple rhetorical craft. Many messages today "work" just because they are beautifully attractive. Aristotle despised vacuous artistry, and much of his book was an answer to an older Greek tradition of a speaker winning audiences through sheer tricks of emotive speech.

That said, Aristotle acknowledged that we are all emotional beings with real needs and individual personalities, and it is a foolish persuader who thinks she can capture an audience by logic alone. Some of our biggest decisions in life—the house we buy, the job we take, the partner we marry—are made with both *logos* and *pathos*. That which is true, argued Aristotle, will also be beautiful and compelling.

But *logos* and *pathos* are only two factors influencing our readiness to accept a new message. There is also a social and ethical dimension that the ancient philosopher called *ethos*. On the speaker's side, *ethos* is her ability to convey integrity, truthfulness and believability. On the hearers' side, *ethos* refers to all of the social factors that influence their willingness to accept the messenger and her message as worthy of trust. It is a simple fact of social psychology that we tend to believe people we like and trust; moreover, whom we find ourselves liking and trusting in the first place is itself hugely influenced by our upbringing, education, social class, circle of friends and so on.

If I told you that I thought you came across as "a little self-important" in a recent meeting, it would probably have limited effect, since you don't really know me and have only a partial feeling about my trustworthiness. But if your closest friend and colleague said the same thing, you are unlikely to dismiss it. The same words may be used by both of us; the same evidence may be presented; but, somehow, the words of the trusted friend are much more compelling. Aristotle put it like this: "We believe good-hearted people to a greater extent and more quickly than we do others on all subjects in general and completely so in cases where there is not exact knowledge but room for doubt."[2] What we now call the "sociology of knowledge" Aristotle put his finger on more than two thousand years ago.

There is a place for an entire book on the relevance of Aristotle's theory of rhetoric. For now I simply want to underline a dimension of persuasion that is obvious once you hear it but too often overlooked by leaders seeking to influence those in their care: *The perceived character of the persuader is central to his powers of persuasion.* This is *ethos* in Aristotle's system. As the quotation above highlights, we tend to accept arguments made by those we personally trust, the "good-hearted". A half-plausible argument will sound implausible from someone we don't like or respect, and yet the same argument will seem fully plausible from someone we deeply respect. Taking a shot at the frivolous rhetoricians of his day who thought persuasion was all about style and panache (*pathos*), Aristotle went so far as to declare that the character of a speaker is the defining feature of persuasion:

> It is not the case, as some of the technical writers propose in their treatment of the art [of persuasion], that good-heartedness on the part of the speaker makes no contribution to persuasiveness; rather, character [*ethos*] is almost, so to speak, the controlling factor in persuasion.[3]

Interestingly, Aristotle makes a distinction in his treatment of *ethos* between the speaker's real character and his mere reputation or authority. One could be an ancient Greek senator or a modern business guru and it would not count nearly as much to an audience or corporation as the perceived integrity and authenticity of that leader. Mere reputation cannot match true character.

How Humility Persuades

The point for leaders is simple: the two key leadership tools are closely related. Persuasion is hugely dependent on example. The kind of life we exhibit in daily speech, decisions and interactions — the kind of character we convey — is almost, to use Aristotle's words, the "controlling factor in persuasion". Harvard's leadership expert John P. Kotter puts it simply in a chapter titled "What Leaders Really Do":

> Whether delivered with many words or a few carefully chosen symbols, such messages are not necessarily accepted just because they are understood. Another big challenge in leadership efforts is credibility — getting people to believe the message. Many things contribute to credibility: the track record of the person delivering the message, the content of the message itself, the communicator's reputation for integrity and trustworthiness, and the consistency between words and deeds.[4]

A military commander who is known to put the good of the troops before his own progress will be able to persuade soldiers to take a course of action that might otherwise seem incautious. A football coach who is eminently fair is unlikely to be accused of favouritism or self-interest when he makes a contentious substitution. An executive who is widely appreciated for taking the time to listen to staff before making critical decisions will gain a hearing from employees when she announces changes involving reshuffles and lay-offs.

I was interested to note the title of the *first* chapter in the classic book *Harvard Business Review on Effective Communication*. It is called "Listening to People", written by Ralph Nichols of the University of Minnesota and former president of the National Society for the Study of Communication.

The chapter opens this way: "Business is tied together by its systems of communication. This communication … depends more on the spoken word than it does on the written word; and the effectiveness of the spoken word hinges not so much on how people talk as on how they listen."[5] A similar theme continues in the second chapter, "How to Run a Meeting". There Antony Jay, former BBC executive, offers this sage advice about the effective chairperson:

> It is the chairman's self-indulgence that is the greatest single barrier to the success of a meeting. His first duty, then, is to be aware of the temptation and of the dangers of yielding to it. The clearest of the danger signals is hearing himself talking a lot during a discussion … If the chairman is to make sure that the meeting achieves valuable objectives, he will be more effective seeing himself as the servant of the group rather than as its master … His true source of authority with the members is the strength of his perceived commitment to their combined objective.[6]

Jay's final statement is the modern equivalent of Aristotle's insistence that *character* is almost the controlling factor in effective communication.

I found this principle working on me when I was involved in a historical documentary for Australian television a few years ago. I had the opportunity to interview about a dozen international experts on ancient Judaism, the life of Christ, the Dead Sea Scrolls, first-century Rome, archaeology and so on. It was a dream come true. At one point the producer described me as "a kid in a candy shop"! All of the scholars were at the top of their respective fields — full professors in leading universities — but some carried themselves more like low-level researchers than renowned authorities. Two stood out.

Martin Hengel was professor (later, professor emeritus) of New Testament and early Judaism at Germany's prestigious University of Tübingen from 1972 until his death in July 2009. The author of dozens of important monographs and literally hundreds of technical articles, Professor Hengel was the scholar's scholar, as comfortable in the classical sources of Greece and Rome as he was in the many and varied writings of Jewish and Christian antiquity. Few experts can expect to write something others will describe as "landmark", but Hengel was a one-man landscape producing standard works in various areas of history.

I had the privilege of conducting what was perhaps Hengel's last full-scale television interview. When the film

Centre for Public Christianity

Martin Hengel during the interview in his home Tübingen, Germany, 2007.

crew and I met him in his flat overlooking the Neckar River in central Tübingen, I was struck by several things. First, his enormous private library was described by his academic colleague Peter Stuhlmacher, whom we interviewed later that day, as "perhaps the finest private collection in Europe." Actually, his "flat" was two spacious, interconnected three-bedroom apartments, one for him and the warmly hospitable Frau Hengel and one for books—at least four large rooms filled to overflowing with scholarly tomes written in German, English, French and Italian, as well as all of the relevant primary sources in Hebrew, Aramaic, Syriac, Coptic, Greek and Latin. During the interview I couldn't help gazing around the room and noticing the countless slips of paper peering out of so many of the items on the shelves. These books had been analysed and absorbed, not just consulted and displayed. I left his home feeling slightly fraudulent as a scholar.

Most of all, I was also deeply impressed by Hengel's humility. He really seemed as interested in each of us—a junior historian, cameraman, sound guy, director, producer—as we were in him. As we enjoyed coffee and Brezel following the formalities, Herr and Frau Hengel peppered us with questions about *our* work, our families, life in Australia and the various other scholars we knew. It is a special kind of person who has so much to give and yet prefers to find out about others. I have since learned from other scholars around the world that the Hengels were known in Tübingen for their Friday evening discussions in the home with groups of eager students. These would often run until midnight. Hospitality, friendship and scholarship always went together in Hengel's life. Meeting Martin Hengel had a peculiar effect on me, but before I describe it let me offer my second example.

Professor Richard Bauckham of the University of St Andrew's, Scotland (recently moved to Cambridge), is a pure polymath, comfortable in eight languages (a few of them modern), author of more than thirty books and competent in adjunct fields of historical enquiry that, I am ashamed to say, I hadn't even heard of before reading his works (*onomastics*, for instance — the study of ancient names, their distribution, derivation and social significance). When our crew arrived at the beautiful St Mary's College, where his office was, we were taken aback by Bauckham's offer of tea and coffee for the entire crew. It's a small thing perhaps, but other than Hengel, it was the only offer of refreshments we received during the filming.

John Dickson and Richard Bauckham at the University of St Andrew's, Scotland, 2006.

What's more, after Bauckham took our orders—tea, white with one; coffee, black, and so on—he disappeared for some minutes. We thought it was to arrange the order, but he returned with a tray, having made them all himself. He handed them out to the members of the crew and then sat down for one of the most erudite interviews of the documentary. At one level, this was a simple human courtesy—nothing to make a big deal of. But it was not common, and there is something beautiful about someone at the top of their field choosing to treat you more like guests than filmmakers looking for a big name interview.

The effect of meeting Hengel and Bauckham was completely unexpected. Months later as I was working on an academic project, I reached over to the bookshelf to consult Hengel on some contentious detail and I found myself strangely persuaded by his viewpoint. Yes, this was largely because of the cogency of the argument (the *logos*), but if I'm honest, it had also to do with my experience with the man. His thoughts on a complicated topic were more compelling to me than those of others, including some of the other scholars I met and interviewed.

I had exactly the same experience days later reaching for Richard Bauckham's recent tome. In it he offers a controversial argument about the way ancient people preserved important traditions by memory rather than in writing (this is called "oral tradition"). I have to admit I found myself more readily convinced by his case than that of other equally credentialed dons. Again, I don't think it is simply because I had met the man, as I have not noticed the same "background credulity" toward all of the scholars I met during the filming. Only when reflecting on Aristotle's ideas about character and persuasion did I become fully aware of the "bias" I had toward agreeing with Hengel and Bauckham. The effect comes not simply from meeting them; it derives from my impression of these two senior academics as thoughtful, caring, humble human beings — "goodhearted", in Aristotle's language.

In *Lend Me Your Ears: Great Speeches in History*, former White House speech writer William Safire tells of a certain fifth-century BC Athenian orator named Pericles. I haven't bothered to verify the story, partly because I don't want to know if it's false, but apparently Pericles, a renowned speaker in his own right, once compared himself to the great lawyer and statesman Demosthenes (384 – 322 BC). "When Pericles speaks," he said of himself, "the people say, 'How well he speaks'. But when Demosthenes speaks, the people say, 'Let us march!' "[7]

Real persuasion is invisible in its artistry; it just moves people. My contention in this chapter is simple. Whether in the military, business, sports or academia, humility is part of what moves people. It is not the only factor, of course — and you'll be glad to know I have managed to find things to disagree with in the writings of Hengel and Bauckham — but humility in the leader does exert a powerful, if intangible, influence on those you lead. This is not rocket science. When people trust us, they tend to believe what we say, and few are considered more trustworthy than those who choose to use their power for the good of others above themselves.

CHAPTER 9

Inspiration

How Humility Lifts
Those around Us

I USED TO SUPPOSE THAT HIGHLIGHTING achievements and status is a key to inspiring those who look up to us. There is a real truth here. Most people like to have heroes. Most appreciate being led (well). So there is, as the former head of Australian Special Forces Jim Wallace puts it, "a natural momentum in favour of the leader." Watching Brian Robson, former captain of Manchester United, inspired me to train most afternoons after school. Listening to U2 and watching them perform live numerous times was a powerful motivator to take up a musical career. Reading the books and listening to the lectures of Paul Barnett, a local Australian scholar, was one of the reasons I turned to historical studies. Inspiration does come from those whose achievement we greatly admire. I don't dispute that greatness encourages greatness.

Humble Heroes

But these statements are inadequate on their own. I have come to believe that achievement and status alone are not where true inspiration is found. It is when our heroes are humble that they most inspire.

To offer a small personal example: four years ago my daughter took up netball, a hugely popular sport in Commonwealth countries that looks like a cross between basketball and European handball. One day during my daughter's first season I happened to be in the same Qantas airport lounge as the Australian netball team, fresh from a game against New Zealand. I ripped out a piece of paper, reminded myself they would never see this fawning father again and nervously approached the team, including the famous Liz Ellis, the most capped player in Australian history who captained the country to victory at the 2007 World Championships. I told them my Sophie had just started playing the game and asked for autographs. The response was wonderful. They quickly set me at ease, introduced me around the other players and filled the page with signatures and a little message of encouragement.

When I arrived home Sophie loved it. The page was quickly framed and hung on her bedroom wall. It was inspiring, not just for me as an eager Saturday morning spectator but also for her. Sophie is now—and I'm afraid there's no humble way to put this—quite a little star in her own right, playing in the State representative competition. Of course, it would be stretching things to draw a straight line between Liz Ellis's signature four years ago and Sophie's quick movement up the netball grades. But this seemingly minor kindness from Sophie's sporting heroes did cause a *lift* in her feeling for the game.

True greatness is marked by a thousand small courtesies like this. The inspiration of heroes and leaders is only enhanced by their willingness to take an interest in others and to talk about things other than their achievements. I note in passing that one of Liz Ellis's two "people most admired", according to her website, is Sir Edmund Hillary. I wonder if it was his famously humble attitude as much as his conquest of Everest that has inspired Ellis herself.

As I mentioned in chapter 1, in recent years business leaders are emphasizing the same thing: humility in leadership seems to have a marked positive influence on individuals and organizations. Jim Collins's famous "Level 5 Leader" is a truly odd beast. Level 4 leadership is what we normally associate with big-time executives. This "effective leader", Collins says, "catalyzes commitment to and vigorous pursuit of a clear and compelling vision stimulating higher performance standards."[1]

But all eleven companies that managed to outperform the market by three times over a fifteen-year period — the good-to-great companies — were led by a different individual (and culture) entirely. The Level 5 Executive "builds enduring greatness through a paradoxical blend of personal humility and professional will."[2] In interview after interview, Collins says, the humble character of these steely-willed leaders was clear, not just in their interactions with

Collins's research team but, perhaps more importantly, in the research team's discussions with employees. Independently of each other and in different ways, workers close to the executive would report how he was unassuming or always courteous or asked questions of others or put the firm's interests above their own. Humility, in other words.

The Aspirational Effect

Why does humility in the leader inspire others to perform their best for the company? Collins doesn't offer a clear answer, but I think there are several reasons. The first is the simple observation made in the previous chapter: humility is persuasive. People find themselves trusting the decisions and arguments of someone who puts others before themselves.

Second, humility in the leader orients everyone in the team toward achieving the organization's key objectives. When employees suspect the leader is in it for himself, they lose motivation or, worse, start imitating him and looking for what they themselves can squeeze out of the organization. This is much harder to get away with when everyone knows that the people at the top are striving for the company goal, not personal glory.

The third reason is that the humble leader gives the real impression that she is a "normal person". The aloof, unapproachable leader seems an alien creature. She is revered and spoken of in hushed tones, but she is not emulated because her achievements seem unreachable. By contrast, the executive who chats to employees, seeks their advice, freely pays compliments and does what she can to ensure workers' needs are cared for—as well as kicking spectacular corporate goals—is far more likely to seem "real" and become an object of emulation, not just admiration. Employees start to like what they see of leadership and begin to believe that they too could one day move toward greater responsibility within the organization. This *aspirational effect* is a key to humility's power to inspire.

The fourth and final reason I can think of for humility's inspirational effect on an organization is that it fosters loyalty toward the leader. Every leader knows that the loyalty of the team can be every bit as important as the loyalty of consumers. It minimizes unhelpful internal criticism, maximizes staff motivation and resilience and leads to lower staff turnover rates.

A similar answer to the question of why humility inspires was given by Jim Wallace, mentioned at the outset of the chapter. Brigadier Wallace started out as a captain in the elite Special Air Service. Some of the stories he tells of SAS training and missions seem straight out of the movies. He moved up through the ranks until he was the commander of the SAS and then commander of all Special Forces in Australia. I recently asked him for his thoughts on leadership after decades in the armed forces. He replied:

> Most people want to be led, and there is therefore a natural momentum in favour of the leader. But what continually gets in the way is ego. Where we can't control that, suppress it, then people quickly realise it's about us, and any natural advantage fades and leadership becomes hard work.

The real power of effective leadership is maximising other people's potential, which inevitably demands also ensuring that they get the credit. When our ego won't let us build another person up, when everything has to build us up, then the effectiveness of the organisation reverts to depending instead on how good we are in the technical aspects of what we do. And we have stopped leading and inspiring others to great heights.[3]

"Leading and inspiring others to great heights," says Wallace, come through *humility.* That's not exactly his word, but it is what he means. The inspiring leader must control his ego and throw his energies into "maximising other people's potential" and "ensuring that they get the credit". When leadership is about us, the organization reverts to mere operational expertise because people stop believing in the goal. The whole is reduced to the sum of its parts. Conversely, where the leader throws his energy into the organization and its aims, he experiences that "natural momentum in favour of the leader" that Wallace speaks of.

What I Learnt from U2

Let me close this chapter with another personal example of humility's effect on me. When I was starting out in my first band at age sixteen, my musical heroes were the band U2. Ever since their 1982 album *October*, these four Irishmen represented all that I wanted to do (next to playing striker for Manchester United): create music, tour the world and move people through passionate live performances. When they came to Sydney in 1984, I had to meet them. The problem was, no fans were allowed inside their trendy, inner city hotel. A friend had an idea: let's dress up in suits, borrow briefcases and catch a taxi to the hotel. Perhaps security will think we're staying there.

It must have looked ridiculous—a gang of five or six teenagers thoroughly overdressed arriving in convoy at one of Sydney's stylish establishments. It worked a treat, though. The doorman peered through the taxi window, opened the door and escorted us straight past the two hundred suspicious onlooking fans right into the hotel lobby. Without a clear plan we quickly made our way to the restaurant on the lower level and ordered the cheapest thing on the menu (coffee and raisin toast, I seem to recall). We waited. Surely the guys from U2 would have to eat breakfast sometime! We were right, but not before the hotel manager spotted us and made his approach. "Lads," he said as we looked up like rabbits caught in the spotlight, "I've been watching you all morning. I know what you're up to. But I like your initiative. Stay as long as you like!"

AP Images

Bono, lead singer of U2, during their Elevation Tour 2001 at the Molson Center in Montreal, Quebec, Oct. 12, 2001.

We couldn't believe our ears—and ordered another round of coffee and raisin toast.

Eventually, the band came down one by one. Bono, the lead singer, took a table just metres from ours. My mates voted that I should go over and ask him to join us for a few minutes. That's exactly what I did, and it's exactly what he did. For what seemed like an hour but was probably no more than five minutes, he signed everything we put in front of him, posed for photos and answered questions— questions about songs, the band, their well-publicized faith, the music industry and so on. The Edge (guitarist) and Larry Mullen Jr (drummer) were just as generous when we pounced on them. Looking back it must have been an annoying interruption for one of the world's most sought-after bands. They would have been well within their rights

John Dickson arm-in-arm with the Edge, 1984.

to fob us off. But they didn't. They were patient, courteous and surprisingly mild-mannered (especially Larry, who blushed when we fronted up to him).

I would have loved U2's music either way. But I doubt they would have had quite the impact on me without this experience. The way they let me and my mates in, gave us time and treated us like equals instead of fawning fans was hugely inspiring. For a moment we imagined that we too could "go professional", touring and recording full time. Sure enough, within a few years that's exactly what we were doing. We never had more than minor musical success, but I can't help feeling that part of the reason we punched above our weight for a decade was a brief moment of humility from our musical heroes. That day helped us to believe that a music career was not just for supermen inhabiting unapproachable glory; it was for people just like us. The inspirational (and aspirational) effect of humility is real.

CHAPTER 10

Harmony

Why Humility Is Better Than "Tolerance"

BEFORE CLOSING WITH A FEW "TIPS" ON HOW TO cultivate humility in our personal and professional dealings, I want to describe a crucial benefit of humility at the societal level. In a morally and religiously diverse culture such as ours, humility is a much-needed key to harmony.

The Danger of Conviction

The recent "new atheists", Richard Dawkins, Daniel Dennet and Christopher Hitchens, have brought into sharp focus the pernicious effect of monopolistic religious and moral viewpoints. Hitchens speaks for many when he writes:

> We believe with certainty that an ethical life can be lived without religion. And we know for a fact that the corollary holds true — that religion has caused innumerable people

not just to conduct themselves no better than others, but to award themselves permission to behave in ways that would make a brothel-keeper or an ethnic cleanser raise an eyebrow.[1]

As I write these words and as you read them, people of faith are in their different ways planning your and my destruction, and the destruction of all hard-won human attainments that I have touched upon. Religion poisons everything.[2]

Often the answer to the harmful effects of absolute truth claims is argued to be "tolerance". If only people would tolerate each other, the logic goes, they would get on. Tolerance in this context usually means something like *agreeing that all viewpoints are equally true or valid.* In an attempt to establish this concept on the world stage, the 48th UN General Assembly declared that 1995 would be the "International Year for Tolerance".[3]

The need for such a year was clear. "Intolerance is one of the greatest challenges confronting us on the eve of the twenty-first century," said the UN mission statement. "Intolerance is both an ethical and political issue. It is a fact that in most societies today, many different religions, cultures and lifestyles coexist. It is essential to recall that the basic human values that unite us are stronger than the forces that pull us apart." The supporting documentation offered a striking set of definitions of the virtue:

> Tolerance is the recognition and acceptance of individual differences.
>
> Tolerance is recognition that no individual culture, nation or religion has the monopoly of knowledge or truth.

> Tolerance is a form of freedom, freedom from prejudice, freedom from dogma.
>
> A tolerant person is master of his own opinions and actions.[4]

What I find interesting about this definition is the way it seeks to establish harmony between people of differing views by asking them to *soften convictions*. Only by rejecting dogma and accepting contrary views as valid can we hope to get on with each other; that is the gist of the document. With due respect to the careful thought that went into the International Year for Tolerance, I think we can do better than to ask people of strong conviction—or even dogma—to relax their claims to knowledge and truth.

The Limits of Tolerance

Think of the religious context for a moment. Can we seriously ask Buddhists to accept as valid the Hindu doctrine of "atman" or eternal soul when the Buddha himself rejected the idea and taught that there is no soul and, ultimately, not even a self? On this logic, "tolerance" requires the Buddhist to accept two utterly contradictory viewpoints as equally true and valid.

Again, can a convinced Christian accept as valid the insistence of the Quran that Jesus was only a human prophet and not in any sense divine? The divinity of Christ has been central to Christianity from the beginning. It would involve a logical contradiction for a modern Christian to accept an idea so at odds with her core convictions.

Equally, of course, there is no point asking devout Muslims to accept as valid the Christian idea that Jesus *was* divine and that he died on a cross for the sins of the world. The Quran explicitly rejects these things.

In a moral context, "tolerance" (as it is usually understood) is equally problematic. Think of the terrible culture wars between the Left and the Right in various Western countries, especially in the United States. What would tolerance mean in the abortion debate, to pick a tricky example? "Liberals" cannot be expected to accept as valid the conservative view that abortion is a selfish destruction of a powerless human-to-be. To be true to their convictions, liberals will reject that opinion as invasive, imperialistic and bigoted. The reverse is also true. "Conservatives" cannot countenance the view that abortion is simply part of a woman's natural right to control her own body. They believe there are much larger issues at play.

To continue my controversial tightrope walk, take same-sex marriage. Tolerance of the conservative view is not an option for a long-term gay couple. How can they be asked to regard as true and valid the claim that their relationship is a departure from healthy historical norms or a sin against God's plan for the family? That said, it would be equally presumptuous to ask conservatives to drop the convictions of millennia, reject the teachings of the Bible and accept as valid a homosexual lifestyle. Tolerance in this sense is illogical and potentially harmful. It is like an inexperienced counselor telling a troubled married couple to ignore their differences and focus on their similarities. This is a recipe for disaster. The skilled counselor encourages clients to be frank about their disagreements and only then to find a way to mend the dysfunction.

Conviction and Humility

How can society as a whole be honest about its moral and religious disagreements and work to mend the dysfunctions? My answer won't surprise you. If humility is the noble choice to hold your power for the good of others before yourself, its relevance in the moral and religious sphere is revolutionary. Humility applied to convictions does not mean believing things any less; *it means treating those who hold contrary beliefs with respect and friendship.*

This is an important distinction. Some philosophers argue that the path to harmony is an *epistemic humility*, that is, only tentatively to claim any knowledge (*epistēmē* is Greek for knowledge). If I doubt my own opinion, so they say, I will tend to be nicer to those who hold different opinions. The argument for epistemic humility—which I regard as a misapplication of humility—runs something like this: observing diversity of beliefs ought to make me reflect on why I believe what I do; such reflection can reveal weakness in the justification for my beliefs or a realization that my reasons for belief are no better than someone else's; all of this leads me to hold my views tentatively and so be tolerant to all other viewpoints.

There are problems with this argument. It assumes that all beliefs are basically of equal value—equally strong or weak. That cannot be. A scientific view of medicine, for instance, *is better* than magical approaches to health. More importantly, since some worldviews encourage harmony more than others do, what would be the benefit of asking them all to relax their convictions? Sure, we might have wished that Hitler doubted his Nazism and Stalin his Marxism, but do we really want the Dalai Lama to do the same? I, for one, am happy for the Dalai Lama to remain dogmatic about nonviolence. The great twentieth-century British literary critic and social commentator G. K. Chesterton made precisely the point I am trying to emphasize:

> What we suffer from today is humility in the wrong place. Modesty has moved from the organ of ambition. Modesty has settled upon the organ of conviction; where it was never meant to be. A man was meant to be doubtful about himself but undoubting about the truth. This has been exactly reversed ... We are on the road to producing a race of men too mentally modest to believe in the multiplication table.[5]

When I talk about humility applied to conviction, I do not mean believing things less. I am advocating that we hold our convictions firmly but do so with a soft heart toward those who hold contrary convictions. A humble Buddhist, on my understanding, can reject the Hindu doctrine of the soul but demonstrate sincere compassion to Hindus no less than to fellow Buddhists. The humble Christian, too, can think Muslims are wrong to deny Jesus' status as divine and his role as Saviour but still work to welcome and honour Muslims as fellow members of the human family.

Library of Congress, LC-DIG-ggbain-06610

G. K. Chesterton, 1915

This should be equally possible in the moral sphere. A humble conservative stands up for what he believes in but never allows his truth claims to become justification for discrimination and bigotry. He regards homosexuality and abortion as profound departures from the Creator's intentions for humanity but actively fosters friendships with the gay community and with pro-choicers and wishes them no harm. Likewise, the humble liberal should be able to profoundly disagree with the conservative position without descending into name-calling, smugness and public bully tactics.

There is a failure of ethical imagination in our culture that probably makes my argument sound quaint and idealistic. We have forgotten how to flex two mental muscles at the same time: the muscle of moral conviction and the muscle of compassion to all regardless of their morality. Secular society no less than religion often operates on a narrow-minded logic: you can only love those whose lives you approve of. You can only be friends with people who agree with you. The logic can take you in two directions. The religious version reduces the number of people it loves — to match the few lifestyles it approves. The secular version increases the number of lifestyles it approves to the point of accepting virtually everything, thus fulfilling G. K. Chesterton's famous quip about open-mindedness: "An open mind is like an open mouth: its purpose is to bite on something nourishing. Otherwise, it becomes like a sewer, accepting everything, rejecting nothing."[6]

In both cases the logic is the same: you can only love those whose lives you approve of. But there are weaknesses in both incarnations of the logic. The weakness of the religious version is its inability to show compassion beyond the borders of its moral convictions. The weakness of the secular version is a loss of nerve about what's right and wrong in the first place.

But there is a third way, based on a different logic. It's where we learn to respect and care even for those with whom we profoundly disagree. We maintain our convictions but choose never to allow them to become justification for thinking ourselves better than those with contrary convictions. We move beyond mere tolerance to true humility, the key to harmony at the social level.

CHAPTER 11

Steps

How It's Possible to Become (More) Humble

Every time I speak on this subject I am asked: How can we *cultivate* humility? Is it entirely to do with temperament, in which case high-D personalities are doomed, or is there a practical path to building this virtue into our personal and professional lives?

At one level we *are* stuck with the personalities we have, so we probably do not all have an equal capacity to become humble. That said, while few of us will fully realize the virtue, I have no doubt that all of us can become more humble than we currently are. In her provocative 2010 book, *The Selfish Society,* British psychotherapist Sue Gerhardt laments the narcissistic trends of contemporary life and issues a call to overcome our worst selves. "Our reptile brain may be rigid, driven by habits," she writes, "with only a very basic social awareness—dominate or be dominated—but we have acquired a whole range of new possibilities with the mammalian part of our brains."[1] I'm not sure about the science of dividing the brain like this but *reptile* and *mammal* are excellent metaphors for the selfish and communal instincts we each find battling within us.

I have six thoughts on becoming less reptile and more mammal in our personal and professional dealings.

First, *we are shaped by what we love.* In a moment I will offer some practical hints and habits designed to strengthen the virtue muscles. Cognitive-behavioural therapy, after all, tells us that thoughts can be transformed by actions just as actions are shaped by our thoughts. But I want to begin by making a more basic point that may end up being more significant than all of my other ideas. It is deceptively simple: *We are shaped by what we love.*

Noticing the inherent beauty of a thing is the first step in organizing our thoughts and actions around it. Loving humility, admiring it and longing for it are what kick-starts the process of being transformed by it. Let me offer an analogy. In my music career I never deliberately set out to sing in the style of Bono from U2. (A quick listen to my songs will reveal that I never quite attained it either.) But that Irishman's lilt and passion, light and shade, left their obvious marks on both my songwriting and vocal approach. I was shaped by what I admired.

Again, I think I have come to possess something approximating an *average sense of humour.* My friends would say this is largely because of my wife. One of the things I loved about Buff when I first met her, apart from the denim miniskirt she was wearing, was her amazing wit and sense of humour. I'll never forget the occasion she offered a candid opinion of clergyman in the hearing of an archbishop. She used the Australian colloquialism, "Pull your finger out and get on with the job"; to which the archbishop chimed, "In my day, Elizabeth, that expression was considered a vulgarity."

"Oh, sorry," she quipped, "I meant pull *thy* finger out!"

Fortunately, he roared with laughter and said he couldn't wait to repeat the comment to his wife. In any case, I have never consciously tried to emulate Buff, but what I admire so much in her has over time done its work in me. As well as not being allowed to take myself too seriously, I would say I now have something approaching an average sense of humour. It's an improvement. She likes to remind me of the transformation whenever I make her laugh. "See, darling, you *do* have a sense of humour!" she says with wry smile. We are shaped by what we admire.

The point is obvious. More important than any of the tips below is the observation that the journey to attaining a measure of humility probably begins with the simple recognition of its inherent beauty. Ponder the aesthetic quality of the virtue, observe it in those you respect and then watch it grow in yourself.

My second thought relates to the first. *Reflect on the lives of the humble.* If we are shaped by what we admire, finding admirable examples and studying them will go a long way toward forming humility in us. There are different ways to do this. The historian in me can't resist urging you to study the great lives and to learn from them. Regardless of the religious persuasions of readers I have no hesitation, for example, in recommending you read one of the New Testament Gospels, perhaps Luke, to gain a deeper understanding of the turning point in the history of humility. As I said in chapter 6, the life and teachings of the man from Nazareth continue to have an incalculable impact on Western culture even where explicit Christian belief has waned.

From the modern era, the biographies of people like Mahatma Gandhi, Albert Schweitzer and Nelson Mandela, as well as those of Florence Nightingale, Rosa Parks and Mother Teresa, will repay close reading. Perhaps equally instructive are humility's counterexamples. Some of the lives of the great CEOs have been written up in glorious detail (sometimes by the men themselves!). Then there are the great historical egos from Caesar to Stalin.

Especially sobering is Paul Johnson's classic *Intellectuals*. It recounts the lives of twelve of the "great" thinkers of the twentieth century, from the religiously fervent Leo Tolstoy to the ardent atheist Bertrand Russell, showing the disturbing pettiness and superciliousness that result "when an intellectual pursues abstract ideas at the expense of people."[2] There is nothing like glimpsing the reptilian extent of human hubris down through the ages to put you off the path of arrogance. Call it aversion therapy. If we are shaped by what we love, it is equally true that we avoid what we despise.

More important than books, of course, are the *people* in our lives who exhibit humility. Reflect on them. I trust most readers will be able to think of a few people around them who hold their power for the good of others before themselves. My suggestion is that you watch them closely, talk to them about their decisions and try to emulate them.

I have benefited enormously in recent years from meeting up with well-known Australian executive and professional chairman Richard Grellman for "a cup of tea" (as he calls his premium Penfolds collection). We discuss life and leadership. He is one of the most generous people I know and, having seen him in action on a high-powered board a few years ago, I consider him the perfect example of Antony Jay's gifted chairman, who never dominates or raises his voice but somehow moves the room by sheer force of character. Observing his interactions with people has challenged some of my own instincts about leadership.

③ Third, *conduct thought experiments to enhance humility.* A thought experiment is an imaginative exercise designed to open up the possibilities of a dilemma and so bring clarity. Historians use them regularly. They use the limited data at their disposal to imagine themselves in the culture they are studying. This helps them to answer various problems, see data in a new light and ask more pertinent questions. We might imagine ourselves as a Jewish peasant in Roman Palestine, for instance, being forced to handle currency stamped with the emperor's image and titles. Suddenly, we can see how ancient coinage functioned as effective propaganda as well as a necessary monetary system.

Ethicists likewise use thought experiments to imagine solutions to ethical dilemmas and to discern new ethical problems that might have been missed by simple rational analysis. One may have a very black-and-white view of abortion, for example, until you project yourself into the situation of a twelve-year-old rape victim. The process of putting yourself in another's situation raises new information and provides a clearer view of the ethical factors involved. It may not change your view, but it will give you greater depth and perspective.

Thought experiments can help develop humility in business and personal settings by imagining humble courses of action in advance of confronting potentially tense situations. Recently, I was at the centre of a difficult professional meeting. I had asked people to consider some major changes of direction and practice, and this was the opportunity for the thirty or so people directly affected to air their concerns. In the days leading up to the meeting I played out various scenarios and criticisms in my mind and tried to imagine how I could respond gently, truthfully and generously.

As it turned out, my imagined criticisms were harsher than the real ones, but preparing in advance like this helped me to respond to each concern without raising the "heat" in the room. It made the night bearable for all parties. More importantly, my thought experiment helped me see things from their perspective and, as a consequence, to attend the meeting far more sympathetic to their anxieties. Any number of professional and personal situations can be assisted by the humble thought experiment.

Fourth, *act humbly*. This piece of advice may sound a little crude and simplistic but it works. Just force yourself on occasion to act humbly. I am not talking about "pretending". I am recommending that you develop the humility muscle by exercising it, even if it doesn't feel up to the task.

178

I said earlier that cognitive-behavioural theory emphasizes the recursive nature of thought and action. Obviously, thoughts powerfully affect actions, and cognitive therapy frequently involves helping people develop healthier patterns of thought in order to shape healthier patterns of behaviour—replacing thoughts of self-loathing with more encouraging ones, analyzing fears so that they seem less powerful and so on.

At the same time, actions also influence thoughts. This is the "behavioural" part of cognitive-behavioural theory. One of the simplest examples is the advice to "face your fears", originally based on the work of psychologist Joseph Wolpe. His theory of "systematic desensitization" basically involves forcing yourself in a controlled way into a situation you (irrationally) find frightening so that the fear is slowly minimized. Anger management can sometimes involve the same approach: force yourself to count to ten instead of exploding, and over time new habits—usually allied to new thoughts—can develop. More trivially, many people swear by the rule: force yourself to smile and soon you feel happier. When you feel like a reptile, to use Gerhardt's language, just act like a mammal.

I cannot claim to know any specific psychological research into humility, but I can certainly testify to the fact that forcing myself to act humbly in some situations has made it easier and more natural for me to do so in others. The busy CEO of a large company may decide to personally greet five junior employees each morning. Before long she finds that she enjoys it, partly because of the reaction it receives, and soon she ends up doing it without thinking. The captain of the football team determines in advance of the game to deflect the praise of the win onto other deserving players. Not only does this lift the spirit of the team; over time it begins to lessen his personal need for praise. The examples are endless. The point is the same. Choose to act humbly, partly because it is often the best course of action anyhow, and partly because new patterns of behaviour can influence deeper patterns of thought.

(5) My fifth tip flows from the previous one: *invite criticism.* Invite criticism from friends and colleagues. This is not the easiest thing. "I am constantly surprised at the frequency with which chief executives feel threatened by open challenges to their ideas," writes Professor Abraham Zaleznik in the *Harvard Business Review of Leadership*, "as though the source of their authority, rather than their specific ideas, was at issue."[3] Similarly, in "Changing the Mind of the Corporation," Roger Martin speaks of the four discernible stages of a company's demise: the final two are "the deterioration of necessary feedback" and "the proliferation of organizational defensiveness" — in other words, an unwillingness to allow and process criticism.[4]

I am not talking about studied flagellation. I am suggesting that within your team — whether military, sporting, corporate, church or whatever — you establish a culture of thoughtful critique. This can be as simple as creating a "feedback box", physical or virtual, where people can air their views. You will occasionally get some whacky comments, so some discernment is critical, but most people are not eager to criticize for its own sake, and sometimes you will come across gems that influence you for the long term.

A couple of years ago I was involved behind the scenes in a large public debate in Sydney involving well-known professors, journalists and a senator. Afterward, my team was invited by the organizing committee for a meal with the dignitaries. I was flattered. Minutes later I found myself down at the posh restaurant and deep in conversation about rarified things. I completely overlooked my other staff. I left them behind somewhere between the venue and the restaurant. At the time, I thought it was just a small communication breakdown. I soon discovered otherwise. The next day one of my colleagues took me aside and gently but firmly pointed out how he and the others felt watching me stride off into the distance with my "new best buddies". He wasn't being precious. He was dead right. I had displayed the opposite of humility, and it was damaging to the team.

The conversation was embarrassing and painful. From the outside it might even have looked unprofessional — a "subordinate" being so forthright with "the boss" — but it was actually an important circuit breaker. Over the next day or so, as I apologized to staff, I resolved to always treat staff like "dignitaries". A new sense of camaraderie began to emerge in this small team. The benefit of the criticism far outweighed the embarrassment and wounded pride of the moment. As I said in chapter 7, sometimes the (forced) humble place is the place of growth.

I am not advocating a horizontal approach to leadership. I firmly believe that lines of responsibility and author-

Used by permission of the Marion E. Wade Center, Wheaton College, Wheaton, IL

C. S. Lewis, 1960

ity ought to be respected in healthy organizations. I am simply pointing out that allowing constructive criticism and encouraging it at the team level is one powerful way to foster a little humility.

(6)   Finally, *forget about being humble.* In offering these "tips" for cultivating humility, I am reminded of something C. S. Lewis, the famous Oxford don and author of the *Chronicles of Narnia*, said about the truly humble person. He insisted that humility is quite unlike the property of, for example, *having brown hair.* It is not something you style in yourself or even especially notice in others. You don't suddenly meet someone and think, "Wow! What dazzling humility!" It is a rather low-key virtue. It often takes a while to spot in others, partly because the truly humble person is not at all concerned about *appearing* humble. He is not thinking of himself at all. Lewis put it this way:

Do not imagine that if you meet a really humble man he will be what most people call "humble" nowadays: he will not be a sort of greasy, smarmy person, who is always telling you that, of course, he is nobody. Probably all you will think about him is that he seemed a cheerful, intelligent chap who took a real interest in what you said to him. If you do dislike him it will be because you feel a little envious of anyone who seems to enjoy life so easily. He will not be thinking about humility: he will not be thinking about himself at all.[5]

Lewis ends his discussion of humility with a typically provocative and sage piece of advice about "acquiring" the virtue. Far from being self-conscious about becoming humble, we should in fact be reminding ourselves of our pride:

If anyone would like to acquire humility, I can, I think, tell him the first step. The first step is to realise that one is proud. And a biggish step, too. At least, nothing whatever can be done before it. If you think you are not conceited, it means you are very conceited indeed.[6]

I was troubled when I first read this quotation, and it may seem a rather negative note on which to end my book. But the more I ponder it, the more I see its good sense. The very first step in the pursuit of humility is to recognize that I am *not* humble. This is excellent news—it means I must be on my way.

Bibliography

Babbitt, F. C., trans. *Plutarch: Moralia*. Loeb Classical Library 197. Cambridge, MA: Harvard University Press, 2000.

Brunt, P.A., and J. M. Moore, eds. *Res Gestae Divi Augusti: The Achievements of the Divine Augustus*. Oxford: Oxford University Press, 1967.

Bryson, B. *A Short History of Nearly Everything*. New York: Broadway Books, 2005.

Carter, J. R., trans. *The Dhammapada*. Oxford: Oxford University Press, 2000.

Chesterton, G. K. *Orthodoxy*. Garden City, NY: Image Books, reprint 1959.

Collins, Jim. *Good to Great: Why Some Companies Make the Leap ... and Others Don't*. New York: HarperBusiness, 2001.

———. *How the Mighty Fall: And Why Some Companies Never Give In*. New York: HarperBusiness, 2009.

Conford, P. *The Personal World: John Macmurray on Self and Society*. Edinburgh: Floris Books, 1996.

Covey, S. R. *The Seven Habits of Highly Effective People*. New York: Free Press, 2004.

Covey, S. R., A. R. Merrill, and R. R. Merrill. *First Things First: To Live, to Love, to Learn, to Leave a Legacy*. New York: Free Press, 2003.

Davies, Paul. *The Mind of God: Science and the Search for Ultimate Meaning*. New York: Simon & Schuster, 1992.

Gerhardt, S. *The Selfish Society*. Chicago: Simon & Schuster, 2010.

Gilovich, Thomas. *How We Know What Isn't So*. New York: Free Press, 1991.

Guinness, Os. *Steering through Chaos: Vice and Virtue in an Age of Moral Confusion*. Colorado Springs: NavPress, 2000.

Gummere, R. M., trans. *Seneca, Epistles 1–65*. Loeb Classical Library 75. Cambridge, MA: Harvard University Press, 2002.

Harrison, P. *The Bible: Protestantism and the Rise of Natural Science*. Cambridge: Cambridge University Press, 1998.

———. *The Fall of Man and the Foundations of Science*. Cambridge: Cambridge University Press, 2007.

Hornblower, S., and A. Spawforth, eds. *The Oxford Classical Dictionary*. Oxford: Oxford University Press, 2003.

Hurtado, Larry. *How on Earth Did Jesus Become a God? Historical Questions about Earliest Devotion to Jesus*. Grand Rapids: Eerdmans, 2005.

Jammer, M. *Einstein and Religion: Physics and Theology*. Princeton, NJ: Princeton University Press, 1999.

Johnson, P. *Intellectuals*. New York: HarperCollins, 1996.

Judge, E. A. "Ancient Beginnings of the Modern World." Pages 468–82 in *Ancient History in a Modern University*, ed. T. W. Hillard et al. Grand Rapids: Eerdmans, 1998.

———. *The First Christians in the Roman World: Augustan and New Testament Essays*. Tübingen: Mohr Siebeck, 2008.

Kennedy, G. A., trans. *Aristotle, On Rhetoric: A Theory of Civic Discourse*. Oxford: Oxford University Press, 1991.

Kotter, K. P. *Leading Change*. Cambridge, MA: Harvard Business School Press, 1996.

Kotter, K. P., and J. C. Collins, eds. *Harvard Business Review on Change*. Cambridge, MA: Harvard Business School Press, 1998.

Leslie, J. *Universes*. London: Routledge, 1989.

Mintzberg, H., J. P. Kotter, et al., eds. *Harvard Business Review on Leadership*. Cambridge, MA: Harvard Business School Press, 1998.

Morris, S. C. *Life's Solution: Inevitable Humans in a Lonely Universe*. Cambridge: Cambridge University Press, 2003.

Nichols, R., A. Jay, et al., eds. *Harvard Business Review on Effective Communication*. Cambridge, MA: Harvard Business School Press, 1999.

Radice, B., trans. *The Letters of Abelard and Heloise*. New York: Penguin Books, 2003.

Safire, W. *Lend Me Your Ears: Great Speeches in History*. New York: Norton, 1992.

Schluter, M., and D. J. Lee. *The R Option: Building Relationships as a Better Way of Life*. Cambridge, UK: Relationships Foundation, 2003.

Schweitzer, A. *Out of My Life and Thought: An Autobiography*. Baltimore, MD: Johns Hopkins University Press, 1998.

Strom, M. *Arts of the Wise Leader*. New Zealand: Sophos, 2007.

Ten Elshof, G. *I Told Me So: Self-Deception and the Christian Life*. Grand Rapids: Eerdmans, 2009.

Walker, S. P. *Leading Out of Who You Are: Discovering the Secret of Undefended Leadership*. Carlisle, UK: Piquant, 2007.

Watts, W., trans. *Augustine: Confessions*. Loeb Classical Library 26. Cambridge, MA: Harvard University Press, 1912.

Wolterstorff, N. *Justice: Rights and Wrongs*. Princeton, NJ: Princeton University Press, 2008.

Notes

Introduction

1. John Dickson, *DISC Classic 2.0*, prepared by Integro Learning Company, 2009. Unpublished (thankfully).

Chapter 1

1. John Ross Carter, trans., *The Dhammapada* (Oxford: Oxford University Press, 2000).
2. Aristotle, *On Rhetoric: A Theory of Civic Discourse* (George A. Kennedy, trans.; Oxford: Oxford University Press, 1991).
3. Seneca, *Epistles 1–65* (trans. Richard M. Gummere; Loeb Classical Library 75; Cambridge, MA: Harvard University Press, 2002).
4. Plutarch, *Moralia* (vol. 1; Frank Cole Babbitt, trans.; Loeb Classical Library 197; Cambridge, MA: Harvard University Press, 2000).
5. St. Augustine, *Confessions* (2 vols.; William Watts, trans.; Loeb Classical Library 26; Cambridge, MA: Harvard University Press, 1912).
6. *The Letters of Abelard and Heloise* (trans. Betty Radice; New York: Penguin Books, 2003). I definitely prefer the abbess Heloise to her priest and lover, Abelard, but those who think of "romance" as a modern construction will be surprised at the intensity of affection in these letters.
7. A recent philosophical and historical account of "human rights", including its origins in Ockham and even earlier canon lawyers, can

be found in Nicholas Wolterstorff, *Justice: Rights and Wrongs* (Princeton, NJ: Princeton University Press, 2008), 44–64.

8. Jim Collins, *Good to Great: Why Some Companies Make the Leap … and Others Don't* (New York: HarperBusiness, 2001), 13.

9. Jim Collins, *How the Mighty Fall: And Why Some Companies Never Give In* (New York: HarperBusiness, 2009).

10. See *Sunday Express* (London) 13 January 1963.

11. An excellent compendium of selected writings of Macmurray is Philip Conford, *The Personal World: John Macmurray on Self and Society* (Edinburgh: Floris Books, 1996), 173.

12. Mark Strom, *Arts of the Wise Leader* (New Zealand: Sophos, 2007), 129.

13. Philippians 2:3–4. Author's translation.

14. www.ibroresearch.com/?p=52.

15. www.pbs.org/wgbh/amex/fight/peopleevents/p_louis.html.

16. Collins, *Good to Great*, 28.

Chapter 2

1. J. P. Kotter, "What Leaders Really Do," *Harvard Business Review on Leadership* (Cambridge, MA: Harvard Business School, 1998), 37–60.

2. Personal email communication with the author (24 September 2008).

3. Kotter, "What Leaders Really Do."

4. Simon P. Walker, *Leading Out of Who You Are: Discovering the Secret of Undefended Leadership* (Carlisle, UK: Piquant, 2007), 16–17.

5. Quoted in Charles M. Farkas and Suzy Wetlaufer, "The Ways Chief Executive Officers Lead", *Harvard Business Review on Leadership* (Cambridge, MA: Harvard Business School Press, 1998), 127.

6. Stephen R. Covey, *The Seven Habits of Highly Effective People* (New York: Free Press, 2004), 18.

7. Ibid.

8. Personal email communication with the author (24 September 2008).

9. Thomas Teal, "The Human Side of Management", *Harvard Business Review on Leadership* (Cambridge, MA: Harvard Business School Press, 1998), 150.

10. Quoted in "Gandhi, Mohandas Karamchand," in *Encyclopædia Britannica* (Chicago: Encyclopædia Britannica, 2010).

Chapter 3

1. 1 Corinthians 8:1.

2. Josephus, *The Jewish War* (trans. Henry St. J. Thackeray; Loeb Classical Library; Cambridge, MA: Harvard Univ. Press, 1965), 5.451.

3. Gregg Ten Elshof, *I Told Me So: Self-Deception and the Christian Life* (Grand Rapids: Eerdmans, 2009), xiii.

4. Ibid., 1. The research is found in Thomas Gilovich, *How We Know What Isn't So* (New York: Free Press, 1991).

5. 2005–2006 *World Values Survey*. For methodological details and raw data see www.worldvaluessurvey.org.

6. Paul Davies, *The Mind of God: Science and the Search for Ultimate Meaning* (New York: Simon & Schuster, 1992). A reliable account of Einstein's quasi-religious views is found in Max Jammer, *Einstein and Religion* (Princeton, NJ: Princeton University Press, 1999).

7. Jammer, *Einstein and Religion*, 122–23.

8. Ibid., 121.

9. See John Leslie, *Universes* (London: Routledge, 1989), 2–6.

10. Bill Bryson, *A Short History of Nearly Everything* (New York: Broadway Books, 2005), 21.

11. Simon Conway Morris, *Life's Solution: Inevitable Humans in a Lonely Universe* (Cambridge: Cambridge University Press, 2003), 20.

12. Philip Conford, *The Personal World: John Macmurray on Self and Society* (Edinburgh: Floris Books, 1996), 206–7.

13. Richard Dawkins, *The God Delusion* (New York: Houghton Mifflin, 2006), 345.

14. Richard Dawkins, in *The Telegraph* (10 May 1995).

15. Dawkins, *The God Delusion,* 361.

Chapter 4

1. "Hillary, Sir Edmund," in *Encyclopædia Britannica* (Chicago: Encyclopædia Britannica, 2010).

2. Gunnar Jahn, "The Nobel Peace Prize 1952 — Presentation Speech". Nobelprize.org. 19 Aug 2010 http://nobelprize.org/nobel_prizes/peace/laureates/1952/press.htm.

3. Albert Schweitzer, *Out of My Life and Thought: An Autobiography* (Baltimore, MD: Johns Hopkins University Press, 1998), 88–89.

4. The story of the Matthews' lives is told in Nancy Cato's *Mister Maloga: Daniel Matthews and His Mission, Murray River, 1864–1902* (St. Lucia, Queensland: University of Queensland Press, 1976).

5. *Footscray Advertiser* (2 April 1887).

6. Stephen Hawking, "Galileo and the Birth of Modern Science," *American Heritage's Invention & Technology* 24, no. 1 (Spring 2009): 36.

7. Quoted in Arthur Koestler, *The Sleepwalkers* (New York: Penguin, reprint 1990), 475.

8. Jim Collins, *Good to Great: Why Some Companies Make the Leap … and Others Don't* (New York: HarperBusiness, 2001), 27.

9. Ibid., 20.

10. Ibid., 21.

11. Ibid., 38.

Chapter 5

1. David Whitehead, "Philotimia," in *The Oxford Classical Dictionary* (Oxford: Oxford University Press, 2003), 1171.

2. Aristotle, *On Rhetoric: A Theory of Civic Discourse* (trans. G. A. Kennedy; Oxford: Oxford University Press, 1991), 1.11.16.

3. Ibid., 1.5.8–9.

4. For the Greek text and translation of the *Delphic Canon*, see Edwin A. Judge, "Ancient Beginnings of the Modern World," *Ancient History in a Modern University* (Grand Rapids: Eerdmans, 1998), 473–75.

5. Aristotle, *On Rhetoric* 2.3.6–7.

6. T. J. Cornell, "Quinctius Cincinnatus, Lucius," in *The Oxford Classical Dictionary*, 1288.

7. For Latin text, English translation and commentary, see P. A. Brunt and J. M. Moore, *Res Gestae Divi Augusti: The Achievements of the Divine Augustus* (Oxford: Oxford University Press, 1967); also E. A. Judge, *The First Christians in the Roman World: Augustan and New Testament Essays* (Tübingen: Mohr Siebeck, 2008), 182 – 223.

8. Flavius Josephus, *The Life* (trans. Henry St. J. Thackeray; Loeb Classical Library 186; Cambridge, MA: Harvard Univ. Press, 1926), 1 – 9.

Chapter 6

1. Readers who know the Bible well may recall the parenthetical description of Moses in Numbers 12:3, "Now Moses was a very humble man, more humble than anyone else on the face of the earth." In our study we concluded that this text refers not to *social* humility (toward others) but to "theological humility", i.e., submissiveness toward God. Moses is being described here as man of unparalleled reverence and worship before his Maker.

2. Examples include: Psalm 147:6; Isaiah 11:4; 29:19; Amos 2:7; 8:4. The Hebrew adjective used in these texts is *anaw* ("humble" or "humbled"), and it is usually translated by the ancient Greek version of the Old Testament, the Septuagint, with the term *tapeinos.*

3. Sirach 4:7 – 8. Author translation.

4. In the Hebrew text the word "humility", *anawa*, is used in "return their greeting in *humility*". The Greek version has the softer "gentleness" (*praütēs*), even though it has "humility" (*tapeinos*) in the first line for the same term, "humble your head before the great."

5. Matthew 5:3, 5, 44, 39 respectively.

6. Matthew 11:29 – 30.

7. Mark 10:43 – 45.

8. Philip Conford, *The Personal World: John Macmurray on Self and Society* (Edinburgh: Floris Books, 1996), 173.

9. Seneca, *Epistles 1–65* (trans. Richard M. Gummere; Loeb Classical Library 75; Cambridge, MA: Harvard University Press, 2002), 101.14.

10. Philippians 2:3–8.

11. For the historically curious, one of the leading scholars working on this question is Professor Larry Hurtado of the University of Edinburgh in Scotland: *How on Earth Did Jesus Become a God? Historical Questions about Earliest Devotion to Jesus* (Grand Rapids: Eerdmans, 2005).

12. Colossians 3:12; 1 Peter 3:8; 5:5.

13. 1 Clement 2:1. Author's translation.

14. Matthew 20:26.

Chapter 7

1. Matthew 5:5.

2. Philip Conford, *The Personal World: John Macmurray on Self and Society* (Edinburgh: Floris Books, 1996), 209–10.

3. K. P. Kotter, *Leading Change* (Cambridge, MA: Harvard Business School Press, 1996), 27.

4. As of 6 August 2010, the episode could be listened to at www.bbc.co.uk/programmes/p008nqh3. A much larger argument can be made that *humility* was at the core of the scientific revolution in seventeenth-century Europe. Peter Harrison, professor of science and religion at the University of Oxford in the UK, argues that one of the principal causes of the whole experimental method—what we call modern science—was a renewal of Augustinianism, a philosophical school that emphasized the fallenness of the human will and mind. He shows how many of the earliest scientists were conscious of their inability to understand the world in all its complexity. They thought of themselves as "fallen" creatures. They doubted their capacity to intuit the nature of the world directly and so devised methods designed to compensate for their intellectual limits. The experimental enterprise, where theories are not just proposed and believed but tested and corroborated, was an effort to "redeem" humanity's fallenness. See Peter Harrison, *The Fall of Man and the Foundations of Science* (Cambridge: Cambridge University Press, 2007).

Notes

5. G. K. Chesterton, *Orthodoxy* (Garden City, NY: Image Books, reprint 1959), 31–32.
6. Simon P. Walker, *Leading Out of Who You Are: Discovering the Secret of Undefended Leadership* (Carlisle, UK: Piquant, 2007), 29.
7. Kotter, *Leading Change*, 180.
8. Yukari Iwatani Kane, "Apple to break silence as furor grows over iPhone 4 reception problems," *The Wall Street Journal* (15 July 2010).
9. Stephen R. Covey, A. R. Merrill, and R. R. Merrill, *First Things First: To Live, to Love, to Learn, to Leave a Legacy* (New York: Free Press, 2003), 72–73.

Chapter 8

1. William Safire, *Lend Me Your Ears: Great Speeches in History* (New York: Norton, 1992).
2. Aristotle, *On Rhetoric* 1.2.4. Author translation. The key word Aristotle uses is *epieikeia*. Often translated "fair-minded", it has the sense of both justice and charity, so I have opted for "good-hearted", though I am aware that no English word quite captures the sense of this important Greek ethical term.
3. Aristotle, *On Rhetoric* 1.2.4. This is substantially the translation of George Kennedy, though I have used "good-heartedness" instead of his "fair-mindedness" (Greek *epikeia*).
4. John P. Kotter, "What Leaders Really Do," *Harvard Business Review on Leadership* (Cambridge, MA: Harvard Business School Press, 1998), 46.
5. Ralph G. Nichols and Leonard A. Stevens, ed., "Listening to People," *Harvard Business Review on Effective Communication*, 2.
6. Antony Jay, "How to Run a Meeting", *Harvard Business Review on Effective Communication* (Cambridge, MA: Harvard Business School Press, 1999), 43.
7. Safire, *Lend Me Your Ears*, 25.

Chapter 9

1. Jim Collins, *Good to Great: Why Some Companies Make the Leap … and Others Don't* (New York: HarperBusiness, 2001), 20.
2. Ibid.
3. Personal email communication with the author: 24 September 2008.

Chapter 10

1. Christopher Hitchens, *God Is Not Great: How Religion Poisons Everything* (New York: Hatchette Book Group, 2007), 6.
2. Ibid., 13.
3. The resolution can be found at www.undemocracy. com/A-RES–48–126/page_1.
4. Ibid.
5. G. K. Chesterton, *Orthodoxy* (Garden City, NY: Image Books, reprint 1959), 31–32.
6. G. K. Chesterton, *The Collected Works of G. K. Chesterton* (San Francisco: Ignatius, 1986–), 16:212.

Chapter 11

1. Sue Gerhardt, *The Selfish Society* (Chicago: Simon & Schuster, 2010), 23.
2. Paul Johnson, *Intellectuals* (New York: HarperCollins, 1996), 137.
3. Abraham Zaleznik, "Managers and Leaders: Are They Different?" in *Harvard Business Review on Leadership* (Cambridge, MA: Harvard Business School Press, 1998), 83.
4. Roger Martin, "Changing the Mind of the Corporation," in *Harvard Business Review on Change* (Cambridge, MA: Harvard Business School Press, 1998), 117–25.
5. C. S. Lewis, *Mere Christianity* (London: Collins, reprint 1986), 112.
6. Ibid., 112.

Life of Jesus

Who He Is and
Why He Matters

John Dickson

"I strongly recommend this study to anyone who wants to re-examine the deep historical roots of Christian faith and to find them as life-giving as they ever were."—Tom Wright

Join historian John Dickson on this six-session journey through the most significant parts of Jesus' life. Filmed on location in Israel, the *Life of Jesus* introduces what we know of Jesus' birth, teaching, deeds, crucifixion, and resurrection. Includes bonus conversations between John Dickson and humanities scholar Greg Clarke that explore mind-stretching issues such as the existence of God, the problem of suffering, and belief in miracles.

This DVD is designed for use with the *Life of Jesus* book, which features a self-contained discussion guide, but may also be used as a stand-alone study.

John Dickson is an engaging speaker and delivers over a hundred talks a year all over the world, including the US. He brings together unique qualities in this DVD and book: expertise as an historian and New Testament scholar, pastor, author, and speaker.

What others are saying about The Life of Jesus

"John Dickson has done a marvelous job of presenting the story of Jesus, and the full meaning of that story, in a way that is both deeply faithful to the biblical sources and refreshingly relevant to tomorrow's world and church. I strongly recommend this study to anyone who wants to reexamine the deep historical roots of Christian faith and to find them as life-giving as they ever were."

—N.T. Wright, research professor of New Testament and early Christianity at the University of St. Andrews, Scotland

"John Dickson is an engaging and gifted scholar whom I am privileged to work alongside in various global settings. His passion for history, keen knowledge of the Scriptures, and ability to communicate are truly inspiring. I am thrilled to see his unique work displayed in Life of Jesus and I know you will find this study equally fascinating."

—Ravi Zacharias, author and speaker

Available in stores and online!

ZONDERVAN®
.com

Christ Files
A Search for the Real Jesus

John Dickson

Who was Jesus—really? Has the real Jesus been so buried by tradition and legend that he is now lost to people living in the twenty-first century?

Historian Dr. John Dickson sets out to discover what we can know for certain about the life of one of history's best-known and most influential figures. In a captivating journey across the globe, John Dickson examines ancient documents and consults the world's most respected historians and scholars. Beginning with the Gnostic Gospels, he crisscrosses continents on a search back through time for the historical sources that reveal the real Jesus—a search for the Christ Files.

Neither a work of fanciful skepticism nor of Christian propaganda *The Christ Files* provides viewers with a front row seat to the facts behind Western civilization's most influential story. Interviews with twelve of the most prominent scholars and historians and access to some of Israel's most important archaeological sites give this documentary a unique authority.

Includes over six hours of extended interviews with the world's leading scholars and historians: Richard Bauckham, Markus Bockmuehl, James Charlesworth, James D. G. Dunn, Sean Freyne, Martin Hengel, Alanna Nobbs, Adolpho Roitman, Peter Stuhlmacher, Christopher Tuckett, Geza Vermes, and N. T. Wright.

The Christ Files book can be read separately from the DVD, but also provides reflective questions to accompany sections of the documentary.

What others are saying about The Christ Files

"Offers a wealth of knowledge of the key issues. Fascinating and accessible. Open the drawer and enjoy."
—Darrell L. Bock, Research Professor of New Testament Studies, Dallas Theological Seminary; author of *Jesus according to Scripture* and co-editor of *Key Events in the Life of the Historical Jesus*

"First rate historical detective work. Highly recommended."
—Ben Witherington III, Amos Professor of NT for Doctoral Studies, Asbury Theological Seminary, Wilmore, KY; Doctoral Faculty St. Mary's College, St. Andrews University, Scotland

"A sober, well-informed guide based on sound scholarship."
—I. Howard Marshall, Emeritus Professor of New Testament, University of Aberdeen

"Don't be misled by the book's simplicity and clarity; it is based on wide-ranging knowledge of the field and on the finest and most cutting-edge scholarship."
—Craig Blomberg, Distinguished Professor of New Testament, Denver Seminary

"Finally, an honest response to sensationalized stories about the life of Jesus. Addresses with refreshing directness the real questions about Jesus' life and death and examines a sweeping collection of sources in providing full and fair answers."
—Lynn Cohick, Associate Professor of New Testament, Wheaton College and Graduate School; author of *Women in the World of the Earliest Christians*

"Informed by scholarship, yet highly readable, this work is a very useful introduction to historical discussion about Jesus. The DVD is superb, communicating the best of scholarship in a way that ordinary viewers can appreciate."

—Craig S. Keener, Professor of New Testament,
Palmer Seminary of Eastern University ; author of
The Historical Jesus of the Gospels

"There are many excellent books on the historical Jesus, but few written with the same clarity and balance as John Dickson's The Christ Files. A breath of fresh air in a debate too often characterized by sensationalistic, headline-catching claims on the one side and fundamentalist naivety on the other."

—Mark L. Strauss, Professor of New Testament, Bethel
Seminary San Diego; author of *Four Portraits, One Jesus*

"Confusion about the historical Jesus is epidemic today. John Dickson clears the fog and explains with scholarly acumen and compelling arguments precisely how we know what we know about Jesus. First rate scholarship with a clarity found among only the best teachers."

—Gary M. Burge, Professor of New Testament,
Wheaton College & Graduate School

Available in stores and online!

Share Your Thoughts

With the Author: Your comments will be forwarded to the author when you send them to *zauthor@zondervan.com*.

With Zondervan: Submit your review of this book by writing to *zreview@zondervan.com*.

Free Online Resources at

www.zondervan.com

Zondervan AuthorTracker: Be notified whenever your favorite authors publish new books, go on tour, or post an update about what's happening in their lives at www.zondervan.com/authortracker.

Daily Bible Verses and Devotions: Enrich your life with daily Bible verses or devotions that help you start every morning focused on God. Visit www.zondervan.com/newsletters.

Free Email Publications: Sign up for newsletters on Christian living, academic resources, church ministry, fiction, children's resources, and more. Visit www.zondervan.com/newsletters.

Zondervan Bible Search: Find and compare Bible passages in a variety of translations at www.zondervanbiblesearch.com.

Other Benefits: Register yourself to receive online benefits like coupons and special offers, or to participate in research.